Resonant Lives

PAUL GREENBERG has been the editorial page editor of the *Pine Bluff Commercial* since 1967. He holds a bachelor of journalism and an M.A. in history from the University of Missouri. He was a visiting Fulbright Fellow in Soviet-American relations at the University of Arkansas at Fayetteville in 1985; earlier he was an adjunct faculty member in history at the university's Pine Bluff campus.

His column is distributed by the Los Angeles Times Syndicate. Among the subscribers are the *Baltimore Evening Sun, Chicago Tribune, Cleveland Plain Dealer, Detroit News,* and *Washington Times.* In January 1990, opinion page editors of many of the country's largest daily newspapers, responding to a survey by *Washingtonian* magazine, included Greenberg among their top ten favorites and ranked him third (after George Will and William Safire) in the "most interesting mind" category.

Greenberg received a Pulitzer Prize for Editorial Writing in 1969. Subsequently he was the jury's first choice (1978) and a finalist (1986) in the same competition. Among his other honors are the American Society of Newspaper Editors' Distinguished Writing Award for commentary (1981), the H. L. Mencken Award (1987), and the William Allen White Award (1988).

Resonant Lives

50 Figures of Consequence

PAUL GREENBERG

Foreword by Irving Kristol

ETHICS AND PUBLIC POLICY CENTER

The **ETHICS AND PUBLIC POLICY CENTER,** established in 1976, conducts a program of research, writing, publications, and conferences to encourage debate on domestic and foreign policy issues among religious, educational, academic, business, political, and other leaders. A nonpartisan effort, the Center is supported by contributions (which are tax deductible) from foundations, corporations, and individuals. The authors alone are responsible for the views expressed in Center publications.

Library of Congress Cataloging-in-Publication Data

Greenberg, Paul 1937-
Resonant lives : fifty figures of consequence by Paul Greenberg;
foreword by Irving Kristol.
p. cm.
Includes index.
   1. Biography.   2. Biography—20th century.   3. History, Modern—Miscellanea.   I. Title.
CT105.G74   1991   920'.009'04—dc20   90-26723 CIP

ISBN 0–89633–153–9 (cloth)
ISBN 0–89633–154–7 (paper)

Distributed by arrangement with:
National Book Network
4720 Boston Way
Lanham, MD 20706

3 Henrietta Street
London WC2E 8LU England

All Ethics and Public Policy Center books are produced on acid-free paper. The paper used in this publication meets the minimum requirements of American National Standard for Information Sciences—Permanence of Paper for Printed Library Materials, ANSI Z39.48–1984.   ∞™

Ethics and Public Policy Center
1030 Fifteenth Street N.W.
Washington, D.C. 20005
(202) 682–1200

To Carolyn
one-woman syndicate and
the most pleasant of companions

Sources

The following books and articles are referred to and quoted from:

3 BORGES—"The Maker" and "The Golem," in *Jorge Luis Borges: Selected Poems 1923-1967,* ed. Norman Thomas Giovanni (New York: Dell, 1972). "Borges and I," in *Borges: A Reader,* ed. Emir Rodriguez Monegal and Alastair Reid (New York: Dutton, 1981). ♦ 4 BRANTON—Wiley A. Branton, "A Black Leader Recalls an Earlier, Different South," *Pine Bluff Commercial,* Jan. 25, 1989. ♦ 6 CHAMBERS—Whittaker Chambers, "The Price Is Right," in *Cold Friday,* ed. Duncan Norton-Taylor (New York: Random House, 1964). ♦ 7 CHEEVER—Susan Cheever, *Home Before Dark* (Boston: Houghton Mifflin, 1984). Review, Elizabeth Hardwick, *New York Review of Books,* Dec. 20, 1984. ♦ 11 FULBRIGHT—J. William Fulbright, "The Legislator as Educator," *Foreign Affairs,* Spring 1979. Jim Lester, *A Man for Arkansas: Sid McMath and the Southern Reform Tradition* (Little Rock: Rose Publishing, 1976). ♦ 14 GROMYKO— Robert F. Kennedy, *Thirteen Days: A Memoir of the Cuban Missile Crisis* (New York: W. W. Norton, 1969). ♦ 17 JACKSON—Nathaniel O. Stevens, "Where Now, Black America?," *Lincoln Review,* Winter 1988. ♦ 19 KENNAN—George Kennan, "The History of Arnold Toynbee," *New York Review of Books,* June 1, 1989. ♦ 21 LEE—Lines of poetry from *John Brown's Body,* in *Selected Works of Stephen Vincent Benet* (New York: Farrar and Rinehart, 1942). Thomas L. Connelly, *The Marble Man: Robert E. Lee and His Image in American Society* (Baton Rouge: Louisiana State University Press, 1977). ♦ 26 MENCKEN—*The Diary of H. L. Mencken,* ed. Charles A. Fecher (New York: Knopf, 1989). "The Author at Work," in *The Vintage Mencken,* ed. Alistair Cooke (New York: Vintage, 1958). ♦ 32 O'CONNOR—Frederick Crews, "The Power of Flannery O'Connor," *New York Review of Books,* April 26, 1990. ♦ 34 ORWELL—Bernard Crick, *George Orwell: A Life* (Boston: Little Brown, 1980). ♦ 35 PERCY—Walker Percy, *The Moviegoer* (New York: Farrar, Straus and Giroux, 1977). ♦ 42 SCHANBERG—*Policy Review,* Winter 1985 (no. 31) and Spring 1985 (no. 32). ♦ 43 SPEER—Albert Speer, *Inside the Third Reich* (New York: Macmillan, 1970). ♦ 44 STONE—I. F. Stone, "An American Anthony Eden," in *In a Time of Torment* (New York: Random House, 1967). ♦ 47 WARREN—*All the King's Men* (New York: Random House, Modern Library Edition, 1953). ♦ 49 WEST—Rebecca West, *The Meaning of Treason* (Viking, 1947; rev. and enl. ed. 1964). On Nuremberg trials, from "Greenhouse with Cyclamens I," from *A Train of Powder,* in *Rebecca West: A Celebration* (New York: Viking, 1977).

Contents

Foreword

Irving Kristol

Who now reads Plutarch? There was a time when an educated person was presumed to have read at least some part of his *Lives*. One thereby acquired a smattering of information, presented in a concise and easily digestible way, about important historical personages—who they were, what they did, what they thought—that made them in varying degrees memorable. Far more significant than such information, however, were the moral lessons that were explicitly at the heart of Plutarch's endeavor. One learned whom to admire, whom to condemn, and why. This was thought to be essential to the formation of the character of young people.

We no longer really believe in the process of character formation, and therefore do not think that either the home or the school or books have any role to play in this process. We believe, rather, that the character of young people unfolds ("flowers") in a purely natural way, one that spontaneously seeks an appropriate form. To act on any other premise is to engage in "repression," to exercise an adult tyranny over the young, and also a social tyranny over the individual. Not only do we no longer credit any idea of "original sin." (Plutarch didn't, either.) We are convinced, rather, that every infant at birth has a quasi-divine individuality that it is positively sinful to interfere with. (The "interference" of abortion is quite another matter, of course.)

The short essay on a "life," of a kind that Paul Greenberg does so beautifully and magisterially, has fallen victim to such prepossessions. True, he writes mainly about contemporary figures, rather than historical ones, and he writes for adults rather than for children. But adults, too, have to work continuously at "character formation," either to improve the character they have or to retain and repossess it. For this enterprise, Mr. Greenberg presents us with encapsulated knowledge about and insight into important contemporaries. Above all, because he himself is a wise man, he guides us to incremental wisdom about people and ideas—and ourselves.

But what is wisdom? Unless one believes such a thing exists, Mr. Greenberg's judgments can be dismissed or tolerated or ratified as a species of mere opinion. Wisdom, in a sense, is surely opinion, though of a special kind. It is opinion that has been filtered through the best minds and finest spirits of past generations. It is the mark of a truly cultivated person—not necessarily one of the most intensively schooled—that he can distinguish wisdom from fashionable opinion. It is a mark of the semi-educated (even though intensively schooled) that he refuses to make any such distinction, which he believes to be purely arbitrary.

Our intellectual and spiritual elites today are, with some notable exceptions, semi-educated at best. This explains why someone like Mr. Greenberg has not received the recognition he deserves. Oh yes, he has won a Pulitzer Prize and other awards, which is nice. But these are tributes to his journalistic talents as a columnist and editorial writer. As a master of the brief, moral essay, he has yet to come into his own. One hopes this collection will do the trick.

The essays collected here really are quite wonderful. I have known some of the persons he writes about and am familiar with the lives and writings of practically all, and I envy Mr. Greenberg's ability to get things just right. He is often critical, but never polemical or unjust. And when he is approving or admiring, one feels that a discerning mind is being—well, reasonable.

If Mr. Greenberg could be persuaded to move away from the contemporary scene and compose such moral essays on historical characters, what a superb book these would make. It would be the ideal gift for a younger person, one that would move him or her gently toward intellectual and moral maturity, and would remain valuable in later years for refreshment and reinforcement. Paul Greenberg really ought to do this, because only he can.

Irving Kristol is co-editor of The Public Interest *and the publisher of* The National Interest.

Preface

The obituary editorial has become an unrelished chore on many newspapers. You can tell by the dull ring of duty in the prose. But such an assignment should really be seen as an opportunity. Endings lend perspective. They teach in a way that beginnings cannot. It is better to visit a house of mourning, a Talmudic sage once advised, than a house of joy. That a skull on the desk as a *memento mori* has given way to the modern office wall lined with plaques and citations is not an improvement. Not all these highly opinionated pieces are obituaries, but each offers Gentle Reader a kind of summing up.

I am indebted to Carol Griffith, senior editor at the Ethics and Public Policy Center, for going through the undifferentiated mass of columns I sent her in a cardboard box and finding a book. Inside, it turns out, were fifty characters in search of a theme. And she provided one: *Resonant Lives*.

The idea of history as biography enlarged has faded in recent times under the onslaught of the social "sciences." As numbers replace names in the history books, and general trends take the place of specific events, something has been lost, mainly the person and the story. "Anecdotal" has become a pejorative term. The moral of a story, now known as the conclusion, has to be expressed in numbers or vague generalities to be respectable. This is not an improvement, either. Something not just of beauty but of great use is being lost.

I am grateful to George Weigel, president of the Ethics and Public Policy Center, for suggesting a collection of my newspaper columns. I'm one of those writers who know a piece is finished only after they've taken out all the commas and then put them back in again. Even then I am uneasy. Every day, when the *Pine Bluff Commercial* is off the press and waiting to be distributed, I glance over the editorials and wish I had the chance to upgrade a semi-colon to a period, or substitute a comma for a dash. Call it loading-dock tension. I am consoled by the realization that, even if I could make changes, I would only wish later that I could go back to the original. It's my variation of what the psychiatrists call Writing Behavior.

Now the Ethics and Public Policy Center has given me an opportunity to tinker with some columns all over again. For a writer, that's like being given the chance to relive one's life. Thank you, George Weigel. I have relished this opportunity, and used it to exchange old infelicities for entirely new ones.

How have I approached my subjects? What political philosophy has moved me? I'm accustomed to an older generation in Pine Bluff thinking of me, with some suspicion, as a dangerous liberal. It probably has to do with my being a wild-eyed integrationist. In the old, one-issue South of the early 1960s, how one stood on the race issue was everything. Now, when I'm a wild-eyed integrationist about the need to increase the percentage of whites enrolled at the local, traditionally black branch of the state university, I find myself suspect in entirely different quarters. The more things change . . .

Readers tell me that I'm unpredictable, not to say eccentric, and that they're not sure from day to day what to label my politics. I myself have never had any problem understanding my political philosophy. I write exactly as anyone would who was born into a very Jewish family in Shreveport, Louisiana, circa 1937; whose parents were both immigrants from Poland; who went to public schools; who grew up reading George Sokolsky and Westbrook Pegler in the old *Shreveport Times*; who noticed, despite his best efforts and society's, how blacks were treated in a segregated society; who spent a lot of time at the family store in the company of a black retainer, guardian, and role model by the name of Henry Johnson; who chanced on George Orwell's *1984* at an early age; who reacted strongly against the conventional gliberalism of grad-uate faculties of history in the 1950s and early '60s; and who settled in the South—or maybe a better term would be "lit out for the territories"—after a couple of tentative and unhappy feints Northward. In short, I describe myself as an "ideologically unreliable conservative." Biography isn't just history; it can be philosophy.

This preface would not be complete without an expression of my gratitude to E. W. Freeman III, former publisher of the *Commercial*, who gave me the opportunity to write for his paper and who originally edited many of these pieces. And I mean *edited*. To submit an editorial to Ed Freeman was an act of some courage, or at least presumption. To get it back with his initials in the upper right-hand corner meant that it had put on the whole armor of thought. Years ago, I ventured the assertion in a newsroom conversation that Ed Freeman was that rarest of creatures, a publisher who was also an editor. Harry Pearson, whose investigative reporting for the *Commercial* is still remembered, corrected me. "No," he said, putting first things first, "Ed is an editor who is also a publisher." But it was the legendary Patrick J. Owens, another alumnus of the *Commercial*, who had the last word, as usual. "You're both wrong," he said. "Ed is an editor who is an *editor*."

My thanks to the current editor of the *Commercial*, Mike Hengel, for his cheerful encouragement as I got this collection together.

As always, I am indebted to my wife, Carolyn. I cannot envision these essays having taken shape without her. When I had a falling out with the syndicate that originally distributed my newspaper column, I asked if she would mind taking it over just until I could hook up with another. She agreed. Seventeen years later, she was able to hand the column and a much larger list of subscribers over to the Los Angeles Times Syndicate, having edited, distributed, sold, and entirely managed it out of the spare bedroom while raising two kids.

Many others are due thanks; I alone am responsible for any errors I may have incorporated into these old pieces made new here and there. I hope you enjoy reading them as much as I have enjoyed revisiting them.

PAUL GREENBERG

January 21, 1991
Pine Bluff, Arkansas

1 Fred Astaire

'Dances a Little'

Fred Astaire danced with a succession of beauties—Ginger Rogers, Vera-Ellen, Cyd Charisse, Rita Hayworth—yet all eyes stayed on him. Men, women, children, all were captivated. Still are. And it wasn't because he upstaged anyone; that was not his style, or his code.

To quote his biographer, Bob Thomas: "He was feverishly competitive, but always against himself." How American. Yes, there was a time when "We're Number One!" was not the national chant, when the national ideal was not to defeat others but to outdo ourselves, when baseball and grace, not football and sheer force, dominated the national consciousness. Maybe nice guys didn't always finish first in that league, but they were supposed to. And because they were supposed to, they could.

The hallmark of an Astaire performance was Elegance. Capital-E Elegance. It could have been his middle name. His movements were direct, understated, almost clipped—the most elegant distance between two points. To a mathematician, the elegant solution is the economical one. And that was the key to Fred Astaire's elegance. His performance was completely free of the wasteful, the workaday, the ordinary. If Gene Kelly was the athlete of dance, Fred Astaire was dancing itself—dancing in the abstract. He might have been born in top hat and tails. Formal dress was his uniform, emblem, synonym, even anthem ("Oh, I'm puttin' on my top hat, Tyin' up my white tie, Brushin' off my tails . . .").

"Our only god was Fred Astaire," Patrick Dennis wrote in *Auntie*

1

Mame. "He was everything we wanted to be: smooth, suave, debonair, dapper, intelligent, adult, witty, and wise. We saw his pictures
over and over, played his records until they were gray and blurred,
dressed as much like him as we dared. When any crisis came into
our young lives, we asked ourselves what Fred Astaire would do
and we did likewise."

Inconspicuous by its absence from Patrick Dennis's list of compliments is the word "handsome." Yet a poll of women who
patronized a New York beauty salon in 1937 ranked Fred Astaire
among the Five Handsomest Men in the World—along with
Anthony Eden, Gary Cooper, the Duke of Windsor, and Leopold
Stokowski. Not bad for a fellow whose face a Broadway critic once
described as "the shape of an upside-down Bartlett pear." Handsome is as handsome dances. Moral: In America, everything is
possible. One can be handsome by sheer effort.

Effort was Fred Astaire's most American talent. His performance
was smooth, light, airy—yet it transmitted depth and ardor. He
seemed to take it easy because he didn't. He had the magic of
certain politicians—Franklin Roosevelt, John F. Kennedy, Wendell
Willkie, happy warriors all. Like them Fred Astaire had a natural
air, yet gave the impression of having earned it.

And he *had* earned it. He was a perfectionist, and one of the
things he perfected through hard work was the appearance of ease.
The ballerina Margot Fonteyn wrote of Astaire's sense of perfection: "It shines through all his work; there is never a trace of effort,
and that is because he had devoted infinite patience to rehearsing
and perfecting every detail. His technique is astounding, yet everything is accomplished with the air of someone sauntering through
the park on a spring morning." Not till he had practiced the routine
forty-five times was Fred Astaire able to roll up an umbrella, fasten
it, and toss it across the room into an umbrella stand on just the
right beat. The forty-sixth try was the charm. It's the only one you
see.

Of course he had talent, but what distinguished him was more
than talent—it was an instinct for how to use and perfect it. His
definition of class was the American one—something determined
not by birth or station or money but by achievement and the way
one carries it. Lightly yet definitely. Like something that didn't

come naturally but has become natural. It is a style that after a time becomes indistinguishable from the substance. An earned grace. A created self. A person *and* a persona.

The most famous description of Fred Astaire was written in 1933 by a studio executive whom David O. Selznick asked to review the unknown young dancer's screen test. According to legend, the verdict was: "Can't sing. Can't act. Balding. Dances a little." Fanciers of Fred Astaire and the wry in general have yet to find anything in the annals of American understatement to surpass that summation. What delights is not the obvious misjudgment but its factual basis. It is a summary of Fred Astaire without Fred Astaire.

So does America strike those observers whose picture of the country is not so much inaccurate as lifeless. They can't sense the music within. They are numb to what animates and perfects. It is as though they saw only outward things—the present without an inkling of past or future. They don't believe in "American exceptionalism," which is a phrase from de Tocqueville (the best ones about America usually are). They see the limits but not the possibilities of the will to be exceptional.

Yes, that urge can lead to tragedy, too. Or comedy. But when it results in the ever dapper figure of Fred Astaire, you get the perfect balance of cavalier and puritan, a uniquely American blend.

June 25, 1989

2 Samuel Beckett

Enter Godot, Exit Beckett

S amuel Beckett died at eighty-three after a lifetime of waiting. He spent it chronicling every moment in a vast, empty waiting room. The result was works like *Waiting for Godot*, which became emblematic of the anomie of an age. Mr./M. Beckett was an Irishman writing in French, which would make a pessimist of anyone. Only he wasn't optimistic enough to be a pessimist. Pessimism can be found only among those who believe in meaning. Monsieur Beckett claimed to believe in nothing, but Mister Beckett believed in humor, else he could not have practiced it so well, so wryly, so enigmatically.

Samuel Beckett also believed in despair, but perhaps that is to put it too positively. Rather, he believed in non-belief. But he seemed to have trouble holding onto his faith in non-faith. He kept making jokes about it.

This non-believer was also plagued by a pronounced heresy: he believed in prose. Nobody who didn't believe in it could write so precisely.

A man who can tease so much out of nothingness must believe in something, no? Even if it is only the arrival/delay of Godot, whoever or whatever he is or isn't. Is M. Godot explaining it all to our late friend at this very moment, or has Samuel Beckett discovered himself only in the next room of the dream, in a different order of nothingness?

"There are no landmarks in my work," Mr./M. Beckett insisted. The phrase could be his epitaph, his landmark.

"Our existence is hopeless," he declaimed. After his death was announced, mourners came to Montparnasse cemetery to place flowers at his granite marker. They must have felt the loss of something. Perhaps his nothingness.

"His work knew no bounds," said fellow playwright Harold Pinter, whose work knows the same bounds.

The French minister of culture (why does that sound like an office the French would invent and the Irish find hilarious?) pronounced Samuel Beckett "an immense writer, exceptionally exacting, who has profoundly marked his century." No response was reported from the century.

Samuel Beckett leaves behind strangeness, humor, and a sparse style that was nevertheless portentous—or maybe portentous because it was sparse. He also bequeaths the Absurd, as in Theater of. Not bad for somebody who claimed to have no hope. If there isn't any, he found any number of substitutes.

He was a Job without the sense of grandeur, which made him very modern. He was a Job *with* the saving gift of laughter, which made him likable despite his philosophy/anti-philosophy/non-philosophy. He made nihilism fun, or would have if he hadn't gone on so long about it. If a Beckett play was about nothing, it certainly made a lot of it. Vladimir and Estragon, the characters eternally waiting for Godot, seem to go on forever. Surely no sane member of the audience has ever sat through the play without wanting to stand up and shoot both, or at least take them out for a drink if they'd promise to shut up—and if they weren't cemented in those ashcans or whatever it is they appear to have been planted in.

Maybe the author wrote of life as a blank because he had too much drama in his own to make up any more. Living in Paris in the twenties, he took dictation for the near-blind James Joyce, copying the last sections of *Finnegan's Wake*. In the thirties, he was almost fatally stabbed by a pimp. He was rescued by a Frenchwoman (the pianist Suzanne Dechevaux-Dumesnil) whom he married and lived with till she died at the age of 89. In the forties, he fought with the Resistance, barely escaping capture by the Nazis and winning the *Croix de Guerre*. What was left to imagine?

In his private life, Samuel Beckett would have made Greta Garbo look like a publicity-seeker. In 1969 he sent a friend to pick up his $72,800 check for the Nobel Prize in literature.

It's been a long wait for Godot, but Samuel Beckett has been an interesting companion out here in the waiting room. Goodbye, Vladimir. Goodbye, Estragon. Goodbye, Samuel. Goodbye. Goodbye. Goodbye . . . but the characters in his play never quite go. Maybe the man had no hope, as he claimed, but he was in no hurry to leave.

January 1, 1990

3 Jorge Luis Borges

Historian of the Soul

Through the years, a man peoples a space with images of provinces, kingdoms, mountains, bays, ships, islands, fishes, rooms, tools, stars, horses, and people. Shortly before his death, he discovers that the patient labyrinth of lines traces the image of his own face.

—J. L. B.

W hen a civilized man dies, civilization itself is impoverished. When that man is also a dreamer, dreaming itself is the less. Such was Jorge Luis Borges of Buenos Aires and Geneva, of Spanish literature and British civilization, of the world and of a world of his own. Mexico's Octavio Paz, with that unerring instinct of his in all non-political matters, said in tribute: "In stories, poems, and essays, Borges explored incessantly and with prodigious and admirable variations that one and only theme: Man lost in the labyrinth of time. Borges did not defeat time but made transparent our mind and our fantasy."

One cannot read his work without a shivering sense of the depths underneath. In a single very short story, less than two pages long, the reader is introduced to Borges's apprehension of the palpable and his power to transmit that apprehension, to his blindness and how he made of it an inner illumination, and to his thoughts on approaching the next room of the dream, his death. The story is "The Maker," and it begins:

Until then, he had never dwelled on the pleasures of memory. Impressions had always washed over him, fleeting and vivid. A potter's design in vermillion; the vault of heaven clustered with stars that were also gods; the moon, from which a lion had fallen; the smoothness of marble under one's lingering fingertips; the taste of boar meat, which he liked to strip with quick, flashing bites; a Phoenician word; the black shadow cast by a spear on yellow sand; the nearness of the sea or of women; the heavy wine whose roughness he cut with honey—any of these could wholly encompass the range of his mind. He was acquainted with fear as well as with anger and courage, and once he was the first to scale an enemy wall. Eager, curious, unquestioning, following no law other than to enjoy things and forget them, he wandered over many lands and, on one side or the other of the sea, looked on the cities of men and their palaces. In bustling marketplaces or at the foot of a mountain whose hidden peak may have sheltered satyrs, he had heard entangled stories, which he accepted as he accepted reality, without attempting to find whether they were true or imaginary.

The story continues with an evocation of blindness:

Little by little, the beautiful world began to leave him; a persistent mist erased the lines of his hand, the night lost its multitude of stars, the ground became uncertain beneath his steps. Everything grew distant and blurred. When he knew he was going blind, he cried out; stoic fortitude had not yet been invented, and Hector could flee from Achilles without dishonor. I shall no longer look upon the sky and its mythological dread (he felt), nor this face which the years will transform. Days and nights passed over these fears of his body, but one morning he awoke, looked (without astonishment now) at the dim things around him and unexplainably felt—the way one recognizes a strain of music or a voice—that all this had already happened to him and that he had faced it with fear, but also with joy, hope, curiosity. Then he went deep into his past, which seemed to him bottomless, and managed to draw out of that dizzying descent the lost memory that now shone like a coin under the rain, maybe because he had never recalled it before except in some dream.

And the story ends with what has been so artfully foreshadowed— the identity of its hero and the mystery that awaits him and the reader:

With slow amazement he understood. In this nighttime of his mortal eyes into which he was now descending, love and danger were also in wait for him—Ares and Aphrodite—because he already divined (because he was already ringed in by) a rumor of hexameters and glory . . . the rumor of the Odysseys and Iliads it was his destiny to sing and to leave resounding forever in mankind's hollow memory. These things we know, but not what he felt when he went down into his final darkness.

To read Borges is like looking deep within and feeling one's mind split between observer and observed, the search and the memory, and watching each door swing slowly open to reveal a door beyond.

To read Borges is to peer into twin facing mirrors that go on reflecting forever. It is no surprise to learn from his obituaries that Borges was obsessed with mirrors. He was always looking for something, maybe himself, and his writings are a kind of progress report on his search.

Is there in any literature a more concise summary of the division between the artist and the person within the artist than his "Borges and I"? In less than a page he explains the dilemma, and learns to live with it, and die with it:

> It's to the other man, to Borges, that things happen. I walk along the streets of Buenos Aires, stopping now and then—perhaps out of habit—to look at the arch of an old entranceway or a grillwork gate; of Borges I get news through the mail and glimpse his name among a committee of professors or in a dictionary of biography. I have a taste for hourglasses, maps, eighteenth-century typography, the roots of words, the smell of coffee, and Stevenson's prose; the other man shares these likes, but in a showy way that turns them into mannerisms. It would be an exaggeration to say that we are on bad terms; I live, I let myself live, so that Borges can weave his tales and poems, and those tales and poems are my justification. It is not hard for me to admit that he has written a few worthwhile pages, but those pages cannot save me, perhaps because what is good no longer belongs to anyone—not even the other man—but rather to speech or tradition. In any case, I am fated to become lost once and for all, and only some moment of myself will survive in the other man. Little by little, I have been surrendering everything to him, even though I have evidence of his stubborn habit of

falsification and exaggerating. . . . And so, my life is a running away, and I lose everything and everything is left to oblivion or to the other man.

Which of us is writing this page I don't know.

The biography of Jorge Luis Borges sounds much like one of his stories, which should not surprise. He was born in 1900, the grandson of an Englishwoman and an Argentine colonel who was killed in that country's civil wars. He would learn to read first in English—under the tutelage of his grandmother. He was the sixth generation of the male line in his family to inherit a form of blindness that developed gradually with the onset of middle age, as he knew it would.

He came to literature before he came to life, he would say. His earliest memories were those of the library and garden; he was raised in shabby gentility on the outskirts of Buenos Aires in a house filled with three generations, old military decorations, and books. Beyond the walls were the street toughs he would later write about at a distance. The family would take The Grand Tour and be trapped by the First World War in Switzerland, where he would return some seventy years later to die. He would begin writing as a kind of superior hack on a couple of obscure Argentine periodicals, then go to work as a librarian when his father died. It was a less-than-menial job, a kind of welfare program that hired fifty men to do the work of fifteen at the Buenos Aires Municipal Library. But the best he would say about the generals who alternated with the Peronists in holding power was that they were a "necessary Evil." He was too kind. He had underestimated Argentina (familiarity breeds underestimation), and the generals proved unnecessary.

Borges was never enthusiastic about any political system; he just knew what he didn't like—totalitarianism, nationalism, or anything else that would not leave people alone. He preferred to call his country the Argentine, a place name, rather than Argentina, with its national overtones. He was no more enthusiastic about the generals' war to conquer the Falklands than he had been about Perón, but he was not much interested in politicking. Giving a lecture in the United States, he was badgered by a young radical— it must have been in the sixties—who wanted him to endorse some particular utopianism. "Does your cause have a flag?" he wanted to know. "Yes, of course," said the young radical. "And does it have an emblem on it?" asked the author. "Yes," said the radical, who was about to explain its deep significance when Borges said: "Then it can't be my cause."

Born into two cultures, if not more, he had as his personal code politeness, tolerance, and a refusal to reduce man to the abstract. "I don't think I'm capable of abstract thinking," he once said. That he was denied the Nobel Prize, presumably because he would not mouth the correct slogans, became an international embarrassment—for the Nobel committee. His manners remained unaffected, his stories continued to tell of wonders and horrors, mainly those in the minds of men. He was sheltered by his mother, who would live to be almost one hundred. To her, he was always El Nino, The Lad. Slowly he retreated, or maybe the word is advanced, into a world of memory and imagination, always refining his view, simplifying his language, till his stories were ever starker, more powerful, more stirring. He saw worlds within worlds, translucent, plain, dizzying, and enlightening.

Borges was fascinated by the tale of The Golem, the monster created by the rabbi of Prague to ward off evil, and by what must have been the rabbi's torment over having made a creature who would suffer, too:

> To an infinite series was it for me
> To add another integer? To the vain
> Hank that is spun out in Eternity
> Another cause or effect, another pain?
>
> *At the anguished hour when the light gets vague*
> *Upon his Golem his eyes would come to rest.*
> *Who can tell us the feelings in His breast*
> *As God gazed on His rabbi there in Prague?*

The loneliness of man was not strange to Borges, who more than once tried to imagine in turn the terrible loneliness of God. His was a strange calling: historian of the soul. Was Borges poet, storyteller, critic, seer? Or simply a blind old man, frail after years of exploration, who had finally reached the center of his labyrinth in time?

What is certain is only that the world is suddenly flat, dismal, one-dimensional in his absence, and civilization and its dreams poorer. *Tiempo Argentino* in Buenos Aires headlined its Sunday edition with the one salient, indisputable fact about the world in the wake of the news: "Without Borges." He leaves us with echoes upon echoes, tastes upon tastes, and marvelous stories that—more marvelous—are about ourselves.

June 22, 1986

4 Wiley Branton

'Peace to All'

His death at sixty-five was news far beyond Pine Bluff, Arkansas, but Wiley Branton's life will always be part of this place, where he was buried. He grew up on the 1300 block of Alabama, the third generation of Brantons to own Branton's 98 Taxi Company. (The 98 referred to its phone number.)

Years later Wiley Branton would recall how as a boy he might find some loose change under the taxi seats. It was the kind of story he enjoyed telling. Deadly earnest in a courtroom, or in any confrontation where rights and dignity were at stake, he never lost his sense of humor outside it. To be a wholly committed advocate—unafraid, unrelenting, unforgetting—and at the same time to be a whole human being—witty, charming, fair even to those who treated him unfairly: that had to be Wiley Branton's greatest achievement.

Of other achievements there was no dearth. Along with a fellow townsman named George Howard, who would go on to become a federal judge, Wiley Branton would become one of the first black graduates of the University of Arkansas Law School. "It was a pretty lonely existence for most of the black students," he would recall years later. But loneliness would prove a light burden compared to the dangers Wiley Branton faced when he chose to take the case of some Negro children who proposed to integrate the public schools of Little Rock, Arkansas, just as if the Constitution of the United States applied to them, too.

Mr. Branton kept a souvenir of those days with him for the rest

13

of his life—a photograph of a large, partly burned wooden cross that had been ignited against the side of a tombstone inscribed "Wiley Branton." The grave was his father's.

"I always carried a gun in my car," he would remember. "I kept a small arsenal in my office and in my home." He needed to. "They burned one cross on my lawn, but after that, they were afraid to come on the lawn for fear of being shot. I think they would have been." He recalled how various relatives kept all-night vigils, and how white neighbors helped guard his house.

Wiley Branton never forgot the morning he heard that Dwight Eisenhower had called out the 101st Airborne to see that the law of the land was obeyed at Central High School: "I must say that I was just simply amazed. I said, my God, what have I started. . . ." He had voted for Orval Faubus in the gubernatorial election the year before, under the impression that he was supporting "a liberal, fair-minded, decent individual." Later he would have cause to describe Mr. Faubus differently—"mostly a politician who played upon racist sentiments."

Mr. Branton would win other landmark cases, and become the first director of the historic Voter Education Project, which changed the political complexion of the South by registering more than 600,000 black voters. He was chosen for the job by Martin Luther King, Jr., Roy Wilkins, and Whitney Young. Wiley Branton always cited that achievement as his greatest contribution to the civil-rights movement.

He went on to work for a couple of attorneys general of the United States, drawing up civil-rights bills and helping to enforce them. He became an early supporter of SNCC, the Student Non-violent Coordinating Committee that integrated Pine Bluff and many another Southern town. He lost his enthusiasm for SNCC when it fell under the influence of Stokeley Carmichael and became a student violently non-coordinated committee. As Mr. Branton put it at the time: "Having fought all those years for an integrated society, I would be just as opposed to an all-black society as I am to an all-white society."

When he became dean of Howard University's law school, then the pre-eminent school for black lawyers, he took pride in its racial integration. He left after five years of remarkable leadership—in part because he would not discriminate against whites. As he explained it: "The university took the position that since it was a historically black school, it could discriminate in favor of blacks. I simply told them they could not do that." He took up the private practice of law in Washington and amassed enough honors to cover several walls.

A couple of years ago, when asked to comment on race relations in Pine Bluff, Mr. Branton submitted a twenty-three-page memoir about growing up here. It was notable not only for its painful memories but for its generosity and hope. He called the names only of those people he remembered doing the decent thing:

> The first time that I ever remember being called "nigger" by a white person who was not speaking in anger, was when I was called just that by a Missouri Pacific ticket agent. Let me hasten to add that it was not Mr. Seamon, who had a reputation for being fair and courteous to everyone. . . . The *Pine Bluff Commercial* refused to use a courtesy title for a black person until well after the war. I can recall a performance at the college by Marian Anderson and the paper refrained from ever saying "Miss Anderson." . . .
>
> When the Pine Bluff Industrial Foundation was established around 1947, I was among the first persons to make a small contribution. . . . One of the Freeman brothers, owners of the *Pine Bluff Commercial*, was present and wrote a nice account about me in the local paper. . . . I sought membership in the Chamber of Commerce and wanted dearly to participate in the development and growth of the city. But I was to be denied that privilege.
>
> I could write pages about the discriminatory practices of many white businesses in Pine Bluff. I would like to point out here that there were always some businesses and businessmen who were as kind and courteous as anybody you would want to do business with. . . . The Huselton brothers ran the Gulf Gas Station at 5th and State . . . Mr. Clarence Roberts and his sons at Pine Bluff Tire . . . most of the people at Smart Chevrolet Company . . . the lady who worked at the counter at Koberlein's Bakery at 2nd and Walnut . . . C. S. McNew, Jr., Clifford Davies, Cecil Hahn, Bill Burroughs, and most of the people at McNew Insurance Company . . . the Zacks and Makrises at O.K. Ice

Cream Company . . . store managers like B. F. Shinkman, Russell Leibenguth, Bennie Baim (a family favorite), and many others.

And finally:

Despite the many shortcomings, I shall always hold very fond memories of the people of Pine Bluff, black and white. I wish that things could have been different so that they could have come to know me and I could have come to know them, and through our mutual support and endeavors we might have created a better society for all of us. I am optimistic about the future and the basic good in mankind.

Peace to all.

December 20, 1988

5 Rabbi

Rabbi Means Teacher

My sister told me the other night that Rabbi had died. That's what we always called him when we were growing up in Shreveport—not even The Rabbi but just Rabbi. As in, "I've got a note from Rabbi for you to sign." I must have been halfway grown before I realized he had any other name.

Four afternoons a week, I would leave Creswell Elementary School and take the trolley down Line Avenue to Congregation Agudath Achim. In the summer, Hebrew school was in the mornings, but always it was in the same basement room with large, gray, translucent windows that let in the light but nothing else—the bright yellow of hot Southern mornings, the fading orange of late afternoon. In winter, when the sun would set before Hebrew school was over, the street lights would come on, and the dimpled glass would magnify the white light until it looked like some giant nova just outside the synagogue.

Sometimes, hating to stop a ball game and come in for class, we older boys would exchange knowing glances. We all agreed that we weren't learning anything important in Hebrew school, not anything that would help us in later life. We weren't studying Jewish history or philosophy or ideas or anything exciting. All we did was recite prayers and translate the Bible. Outside class we had some pretty intellectual discussions, Darryl Goldberg and Joel Spira and Leon Brainis and Nathan Fox and I, and it seemed perfectly reasonable to conclude that Hebrew school was a waste of time. We knew better than to try this idea on our parents.

17

We called it Hebrew school only formally. The real name is *cheder*—Hebrew for little room. Year by year, everything else I learned in those years, valuable and not so, dwindles a little more in comparison with what I learned in that little room.

I thought of Rabbi not long ago (I often do) when I read about the computerized connection being established between Yeshiva University in New York and Bar-Ilan University in Israel. According to the press release: "Twelve centuries of Rabbinic responsa—authoritative replies to questions on Jewish law and social problems—stored in a computer facility will be beamed via satellite to Yeshiva University in a new $1 million project." A student in New York can now punch a button at a "Responsa computer terminus" and, via a space satellite, have the memory bank at Bar-Ilan "search its data base" for all relevant information contained in "24,000 Responsa—a total of 24 million words in Hebrew and Aramaic—and utilize the satellite to transmit its information to the Yeshiva University computer for an analysis and printout."

At last report, there were only some 476,000 responsa left to program into the Yeshiva–Bar Ilan network, or an estimated 476 million words. I wondered if, once the programming was complete, someone sitting at a screen in New York could extract anything like what was available to a grimy kid sitting in a little room in Shreveport, Louisiana, circa 1950.

When I was five, Rabbi taught me *Aleph-bes*, the Hebrew alphabet. When I was thirteen, he taught me the chant for the *Haftorah*, the Prophetic reading expected of the bar mitzvah boy, and even part of that week's Torah portion, the part of the Bible read directly from the Scroll. In between, he taught his students to sound each word, each syllable; never to pray hurriedly but to pray with *intention*; to be careful and deliberate in judgment; and to greet all with a cheerful countenance.

I cannot say that I learned all these things, but I will witness that Rabbi taught them, year after year. He taught them without an ounce of flash, the same way he sermonized, taking great care neither to delete anything from the teaching nor to add anything to it. He never delivered any explicit sermon against the gods of the outside world—success, power, upward mobility—for he cleaved to the text and the commentaries. That those outside deities were of a lesser order was implicit in everything he did, even in the purposeful way he walked to and from the synagogue on Sabbaths and holidays. He moved with intention. He had somewhere to go.

Asked even a simple question about Jewish law or ritual, Rabbi would always pause before answering. This was important. And on hearing his answer—clear, careful, considered, usually with authority cited—one realized that no question is simple. He conversed with children as seriously as he did with adults, perhaps more so. He had a formal manner but a weakness for corny jokes.

Much is written today about the need for educational reform. Often passed over in the quest for new concepts, new approaches, new techniques are some basic truths: that there is no substitute for time, years of it; that a sense of community reinforces, challenges, and thereby shapes inner values; that there is no teaching without a *teacher*—which is what "rabbi" means.

I was grieved to learn of the death of Rabbi Leo Brener. But I realized on hearing the news that I was far, far more grateful—for his presence, for his presence even now. Almost fifty years have passed since I clambered onto a chair and Rabbi first pointed out the black squiggly letters on the white page. They still resemble nothing so much as a tree of life.

September 11, 1989

6 Whittaker Chambers

Witness

After a time one grows accustomed to missing the dead. And then a name will bob up in the current of events, and absence is suddenly sharpened. "Key Hiss Witness to Get Medal" was the one-column headline over the wire story deep inside the daily paper. "Whittaker Chambers," it began, "the late ex-Communist whose testimony made him a symbol of the McCarthy era and helped convict Alger Hiss, is among thirteen men and one woman who will be awarded the Medal of Freedom, the country's highest civilian honor. . . ."

The account in the *New York Times*, the country's unofficial paper of record, didn't offer much more: "President Reagan today announced the posthumous award of the Medal of Freedom, the Government's highest civilian award, to Whittaker Chambers, the professed Soviet agent who became a celebrated anti-Communist thirty years ago. . . . Mr. Chambers, who died July 9, 1961, confronted Alger Hiss, a former State Department official, before a Congressional hearing in 1948 and testified that they both were involved in espionage for the Soviet Union. Mr. Hiss eventually went to prison, and Mr. Chambers became a hero of the conservative movement and an anti-Communist writer."

After two trials and four decades, the good gray *Times* was still withholding judgment: Whittaker Chambers was a "professed" Soviet agent who became an "anti-Communist writer." If a catalogue of newsmakers is ever compiled in *Times*ese, doubtless Whittaker Chambers will appear under the heading "Communist, Ex-."

20

Or perhaps "Writer, Anti-Communist." But he will not be found under the simpler title he chose, and earned, and gave to one of the great biographies of American political history: *Witness*.

It has become the fate of Whittaker Chambers, a man of many levels, to be associated with one trial and one event in American history, and to be described in one-dimensional terms.

The newspaper stories don't say that he was a gifted writer, period. Or that the description applies whether he was writing on Communism, or the Book of Jonah, or his family farm, or on writing. ("The basic problem of writing is one of creating a kind of order. This runs counter to a popular notion that writing consists in working felicitously with words. . . . If the labor succeeds, if a vision of truth evolves, it will have its own resonance—what the poetry of common speech calls the 'ring of truth.' That tone no art of words can add. It comes from within and instantly marks its distance from the eloquence of rhetoric which is an eloquence of the surface.")

The newspaper stories don't say that Whittaker Chambers was a gifted *reader*, too, with a fine instinct for the core of literature, especially political literature. They don't say that the essence of his sensibility was poetic, not political—which may be why his comments on the prosaic political maneuvers of his time may sound dated now, while his basic themes echo even more powerfully.

The newspaper stories don't say that Whittaker Chambers could sit down to watch a television quiz show in the fifties ("The Price Is Right") and capture the genre in a single paragraph:

"Aaah!" breathes the studio audience, deep from its collective diaphragm. "Ohhhh!" and (rising in pitch) "Ooooh!" they thrill, as if this were the First Day, as if they had just heard pronounced (offstage) the great words, *Fiat lux* and, peeping into the abyss, were watching the Earth take form from chaos. In fact, some kind of revolving partition has turned, or heavy curtain parted, bringing into view several acres of Oriental rug, tacked the length of a wall, or a mountainous display of silverware or Lalique glass; or the latest model of archducal automobile. . . .

The news stories don't let on that, having summed up quiz show-ism in prose that prefigured Tom Wolfe's on slightly appalling subjects, Whittaker Chambers could go on to draw the moral required:

A civilization is justified in seeking to buy survival by sharing its material prosperity with a restive world—like any other form of endangered life trying to save itself. But a civilization which supposes that what it chiefly has to offer mankind is more abundant bread—that civilization is already half-dead. Sooner or later it will know it as it chokes on a satiety of that bread by which alone man cannot live. It will, in all probability, know it before long. For it seems to be a law of life and of history that societies in which the pursuit of abundance and comfort has displaced all other pursuits in importance soon cease to be societies. They become prey. They fall to whatever power can rally the starving spirit of man even though the rallying faith is demonstrably worse than the soft complacency that would suffocate the spirit in abundance. The fall is more certain because a failure of spirit leads invariably by some inward influence to a failure of intelligence.

Even now the words toll.

The newspapers don't say that originally Whittaker Chambers intended to call his memoirs *The Losing Side*. He defected from the Party sure that its cause would win. Yet he would deliberately choose defeat over such a victory. And in that lay his victory.

The newspapers don't say that, having ceased to believe that the West would defend its values, he himself could not cease believing in those values. It was Whittaker Chambers who found the perfect metaphor for the strength of hope in the face of the darkest forces: "When a boy, I was stopped as by a miracle the first time I actually saw how a mushroom, so soft that a baby could mash it by closing his fingers on it, will, in its effort to reach light and fulfill the meaning of its life, force up a slab of concrete."

It would have been enough if Whittaker Chambers had joined the side of freedom convinced it would win, rather than feeling sure it would lose.

It would have been enough if he had written only *Witness*, a book that ought to be required reading in these ideologically ignorant, historically amnesiac times.

It would have been enough if he had left the Party without

writing a masterpiece that illumines not only Communism but good and evil. (It was André Malraux who, after reading *Witness*, noted that Whittaker Chambers had not come back from Hell with empty hands.)

What, one wonders, would rambling, shambling old Whittaker Chambers have to say about being awarded a Medal of Freedom at a White House luncheon? What would he make of the whole, borrowed notion of Medals of Freedom, with their tinny echo of France's Legion of Honor and Her Majesty's honors list? The whole ceremony is as American as replacing May Day with Law Day, or putting shakos on the White House honor guard (an idea that was one of Richard Nixon's lesser indiscretions). If only Whittaker Chambers were around for the Medal of Freedom luncheon, his description of the occasion might rank with his review of "The Price Is Right."

One grows accustomed to missing the dead. And then a name will bob up in the current of events, and absence is suddenly sharpened.

March 17, 1984

7 John Cheever

Lost in a Wood

The reviews were mixed but the book was irresistible. It was a
memoir of the writer John Cheever by his daughter Susan,
interspersed with excerpts from his journals. The experience of
reading the book turned out to be like the reviews: mixed. It was a
bit like eavesdropping on a family quarrel that occasionally broke
off into moments of still beauty and moving silence.

There were times when one wanted to hear no more, for decency's sake. No more about the writer's bouts with alcoholism,
promiscuity, homosexuality, guilt; no more about his disrupted
childhood, his money troubles (which seemed to be of two kinds—
either too much or too little), his temper tantrums; no more about
his daughter, for this turns out to be something of a biography of
her, too. A line keeps coming to mind that Faulkner is supposed to
have said to his quite different daughter when she was trying to
interrupt one of his heroic binges: "Nobody remembers Shakespeare's daughter."

I kept turning pages, feeling like an intruder, hoping to find
more of John Cheever and less of the detritus of his life. Sure
enough, though not often enough, the sound of his words occasionally broke through, like a slant of yellow light through the
clouds of a gray, dying afternoon. As in this passage from his
journals:

> You have been lost in a wood. When you realize that you are lost
> the mind is instantly animated with a kind of stoic cheerfulness.

24

How much worse it could be, you think. You have warm clothes, dry matches, and half a cup of water left in the canteen. If you have to spend two or three days out you will surely survive. You must avoid panic. You must keep your eyes and your mind in the most accommodating and relaxed condition. Within an hour your calmness is rewarded. There is the trail! A new kind of blood seems suddenly to be let into your heart. Your strength and your mind are refreshed and off you go. . . . If you keep to a decent pace, you will be back to the shore where the boat is by dark. You hold to the pace. You keep your eye sharply on the thread of trail. You do not stop. . . . You hike until the end of the afternoon and seeing that the light has begun to go you stop to see if you can pick out the noise of the waves that you should, by now, be able to hear. The place where you stop seems to be familiar. You have seen that dead oak before, that wall of rock, that stump. Then you look around. There is that heavy creel that you discarded at noon. You are back at the point where you discovered that you were lost. The lightness of your heart . . . was illusory. You are lost; and it is getting dark. . . . This is the situation in which I find too many of my characters. I never seem to be able to bring them out of the woods on the one hand, or to transform the world into a forest.

That's John Cheever on John Cheever, going to the still heart of his stories with greater economy and lucidity than a dozen oh-so-weighty critics. The passage is also something of a paradigm of modern man—lonely, knowing that something is missing, fitfully full of false elation, hollow in his self-assurance, searching for the spiritual but unwilling or unable to recognize the Spirit.

"Existential" is the unfortunate word sometimes used for that condition. Walker Percy evoked the Southern version of this same modern anomie in his first novel, *The Moviegoer*, and spent the rest of his life elucidating it. But to explain this unstated feeling is to destroy it. John Cheever evoked it in story after story, and spottily in his novels, though his accent is that of a displaced Connecticut Yankee. There is a wistfulness in his writing, a detachment, a sense of courtesy and nostalgia that the snap terms used to describe the modern predicament—like "alienation"—do not call up.

Yes, perhaps someone should have chronicled John Cheever's incontinences in order to give posterity some idea of the chaotic materials out of which he fashioned his art and his discreet, courteous, white-collar cry from the depths. But perhaps it should not have been his daughter, who is at once too much of an intimate to be objective and too objective to offer an intimate view. The result is a catalogue of childhood grievances and pop psychoanalyses lightened by an occasional filial piety. And the whole unsteady structure is shattered by quiet luminosity whenever John Cheever emerges briefly to speak for himself.

"The angriest I can remember him being in recent years," Susan Cheever writes,

> was during a conversation we had about Saul Bellow's novel *Humboldt's Gift*, which was published in 1975. After I had read and admired the book, I was fascinated to hear through the literary grapevine that it was based on Bellow's experiences at Princeton, and that the main character was drawn from the poet Delmore Schwartz. I couldn't wait to tell my father, but instead of being interested, he was furious. "That's the kind of speculation I abhor," he said. When he was angry, his voice got cold and sharp and he used old-fashioned language. "The book is a great work of fiction, it cannot be reduced to gossip."

Nor can the writer himself.

With exquisite tact, Elizabeth Hardwick in the *New York Review of Books* describes Susan Cheever's words as "elegiac candor":

> The commemorative aspect is suitable to the recent death, 1982, of this extraordinary man and to the pain of family grief. The candor is suitable perhaps to where the culture is now in matters of lapidary inscription. Candor has come to be the sum of the duties attending the documentation of lives by biography or by the reflections of autobiography. Weakness, temptation, indiscretion, infirmity—it must be said these are interesting.

Others might say they are dreary, narrow, and largely irrelevant to John Cheever's art, as far from central to his stories as the inert clay is to the finished sculpture. Maybe this impression results from a conviction that John Cheever would share, and came to epitomize. It is a bias in favor of leaving certain things unspoken—not unclear, just unspoken. And it is a bias that should be indulged in from time to time in honor of his memory.

January 9, 1985

8 Sam Ervin

Vision and Blind Spot

The distinguished senator from North Carolina used to describe himself as a "country lawyer." That is not an uncommon ploy at the bar or in politics, and probably dates back at least to Abe Lincoln's time. In Sam Ervin's case, the description fit. He *was* a country lawyer—with a country lawyer's shrewdness, knowledge of people, showmanship, and false humility.

But of course Sam Ervin was much more, as he demonstrated whenever a question about civil liberties arose in the Senate of the United States. Whether the subject was government-issue prayer or an American's right to be left alone (privacy, for short) he knew the law, and would demonstrate as much down to the last jot and tittle, usually of the Constitution of the United States.

Sam Ervin quoted Shakespeare and the King James Bible, but he *lived* in the Constitution. He came to know its heights and hollows, highways and byways, the way he knew the mountain country around Winston-Salem. It was clear he loved it all, just as he did the land and feel of his native state. North Carolina has mountains and tidewater. Sam Ervin came from the foothills; he had a mountaineer's love of individuality, and deep suspicion of government and all other forms of social organization. That approach would serve his country well when it came time to be deeply suspicious of government under King Richard.

Senator Ervin achieved his apotheosis in the Watergate hearings, which were not nearly as complicated as many another issue he had addressed in his long vocation, and avocation, as a constitutional lawyer. He was one of the few remaining figures in the Senate that justified its old description as the World's Greatest Deliberative Body, a phrase now used only ironically or ceremonially. When it came to the Constitution, Sam Ervin's interpretation could be dubious, or eccentric, but it would be based on sound knowledge. That was the great difference between Senator Ervin and some new "experts" on the Constitution who seem to make it up as they go along, or get their law from the kind of pamphlets you used to find in John Birch Society bookstores.

When Sam Ervin took the Senate floor to discuss a constitutional question, the place would begin to fill as those of his colleagues who could still tell quality would arrive—not to debate, but to listen and learn. For a brief moment, some of the old grandeur of the place returned, and a listener could believe that here, once upon a time, before polls replaced politics and PACs supplanted reasoned discourse, Daniel Webster and John C. Calhoun had debated the future of the Union, while Henry Clay tried to hold it together with small print and sentiment.

A third-rate burglary in connection with a fourth-rate cover-up was no challenge for a man of Sam Ervin's parts; he was in his glory as chairman of the Watergate committee. That scandal demonstrated how smoothly the constitutional processes still work in this country. What might have proved a crisis elsewhere was handled almost routinely, just as the framers of the Constitution may have intended when they devoted only a few lines to impeachment.

The founders of the Republic designed a remarkable machine in 1787, but it is not automatic. It requires people like Sam Ervin to set it in motion, to bring out the facts, and above all to capture the attention of the sovereign in this country—the people. Learned Hand said it: "Liberty lies in the hearts of men and women; when it dies there, no constitution, no law, no court can save it; no constitution, no law, no court can even do much to help it." Sam Ervin and his committee sounded the alarm and roused the people. The constitutional works were set in motion. The country would have been indebted to him even if he had done nothing but preside over that one juncture in the country's constitutional history.

Yet in Sam Ervin's shining vision of the Constitution there was a blind spot. His zeal for civil liberties was balanced by an aversion to civil rights—as if there were a difference between the two. This scholar who could spot a violation of individual rights quicker than you can say Thomas Jefferson couldn't see what was wrong with a vicious system of racial segregation and discrimination that made a sham of the individual rights of millions. Together with the other senators from the Old Confederacy (with the honorable exceptions of Estes Kefauver, Albert Gore, and, yes, Lyndon Johnson) he balked at recognizing that black Americans, too, had civil rights. And year after year he would lend his support to a cause that didn't deserve it, alongside colleagues like J. William Fulbright of Arkansas. So has racism, or at least its political influence, traditionally distorted the judgment of those considered the South's best and brightest.

For some time Senator Ervin couldn't bring himself even to endorse *Brown* v. *Board of Education*, the historic Supreme Court decision that overthrew the essentially fraudulent doctrine of Separate But Equal. And he must have opposed just about every civil-rights bill introduced during his two decades in the Senate. Sam Ervin knew his Constitution; he just wasn't about to understand it on this subject. Perhaps he felt he couldn't afford to, not if he wanted to be re-elected. Whatever the reason, Senator Ervin would fail the great moral test of Southern politics.

The law, Edmund Burke once said, sharpens the mind by narrowing it. And after thinking on the life and times of Sam Ervin, one might add: and by narrowing human sympathies. Sam Ervin may have been wiser than he knew when he described himself as a country lawyer, complete with an unsurpassed zeal for individual rights and a sadly parochial vision of them. In a way, there were two Sam Ervins. There is much to appreciate in his long career, and much to apprehend.

May 5, 1985

9 Orval Faubus

A Trip in Time

We were driving to Little Rock to hear Orval Faubus. Just like the old days. But everything was wrong, or anyway different. This wasn't a snaky two-lane obstacle course but a four-lane expressway. The most overpromised and underbuilt road in the state finally had been completed—long after Orval Faubus (who had done much of the promising) had left the scene. Several New Souths had come and gone since then. The Governor's Mansion had been handed over to a succession of moderates, and there hadn't been a hard edge to state politics for years.

Now we were headed for Little Rock to stir up all those old memories, and grudges. The press had been invited to preview a television documentary on the life and times of O. E. Faubus, Eternal Incumbent, Peerless Leader, and footnote in American history books under Law, Defiance of. I felt like Jack Burden in *All the King's Men*, assigned to turn over rocks and poke into the malice of time once more. (Thus literature robs experience of its original perception, replacing it with somebody else's art.) And like Jack Burden toward the end of Willie Stark's saga, I wasn't looking forward to the job. It wasn't fun any more; it was a history assignment.

But when anybody begins explaining How It Really Was, somebody else needs to be around to see that the footnotes aren't misplaced. He who is allowed to control the present, as any revisionist historian knows, controls the past, and he who controls the past shapes the future. History isn't just a quasi-science, and it's more than an art; it's a political weapon.

At the television station, it was like a subdued opening night, with a small bar, old friends, a comfortable board room with cushy chairs and an outsize screen on which to watch the show. And there was Orval Faubus, chatting amiably. When the hurlyburly's done, when the battle's lost and won, we'll all get together and have a drink. History, where is thy sting?

The scenes from the documentary were almost as comfortable. Nothing testifies to the unchanging mutability of human affairs so much as old photographs. Most of the documentary had the depth of a travelogue, and it came swathed in music that might have been written expressly for organists in all-you-can-eat buffeterias. It sounded both ominous and confectionary. It sounded like—yes, it *was*—the theme from the movie *Jaws* somehow rendered toothless.

The old adrenalin didn't start to flow till well into this candy-coated production. That's when the Orval Faubus up there on the screen was saying: "I think that's part of the proof that the American dream is still possible." He was talking about his own rise in politics, not his part in denying that dream to a whole race of Americans. Then the unlined Orval Faubus of 1957 was telling an incredibly young Mike Wallace in a television interview that the troops he had just called out to bar black students from Central High "will not act as segregationists or integrationists." They were there, you see, only to keep the peace. Law and order would be maintained by having the proper authorities do the mob's bidding.

As for those troops that enforced the law of the land when he wouldn't, Governor Faubus made them sound like some foreign legion. There he was in a newsreel of the time telling the local populace: "We are now an occupied territory."

For a brief moment, just what Orval Faubus stood for in 1957 came rushing back, along with the worldwide name he gave Little Rock that year. Then the lights came on, and it was 1980 again, and I was seated next to a seventy-year-old man who was nibbling peanuts, reminiscing about old times, and rubbing his hands together as he explained why he had retired to Houston. "I've always suffered from cold weather," this Orval Faubus was saying. Besides,

Houston has a lot of medical facilities. He talked of his two recent operations and the medication he takes for his heart.

The old passion faded out almost as quickly as the television screen had. In his last two times out in the gubernatorial races, Orval E. Faubus hadn't done much better than Frank Lady or Monroe Schwarzlose. He was scarcely a clear and present danger now. The second volume of his memoirs was being published by Democrat Printing and Lithographing Co. in Little Rock, which ain't exactly Harper & Row.

This Orval Faubus was repeating all the old lines, unchanged since 1957, but they no longer inspired anger. Only a certain tiredness. It is wearying to be in the presence of history's condemned, and not just because they keep repeating their brief, but because they cannot even enter a room without dragging all that irrevocable history after them, filling every space with suffocating judgment. Their unchanged stance, like an old photograph, brings home how much everything else has changed.

The sneak preview is over now, but Orval Faubus is still going strong, surrounded by reporters, rehashing old campaigns, reaching back for the names of old friends and foes. He still enjoys the game. He will yet justify the unjustifiable, if only history will listen. He'll look better, he said, "in the perspective of history when animosities and prejudices have faded with time. . . ." It is another great quote from a politician who used animosities and prejudices so adroitly, and won six terms as governor. Twelve years in office.

That seemed a long time then. Now it is the shortest, like yesterday when it is past. Stepping outside into the fresh air, I am struck again at this season by how suddenly it gets dark.

November 6, 1980

10 Elizabeth Freeman

Epitaph for a Lady

Life around the newspaper I work for is never going to be quite the same without her. She was Elizabeth Council Freeman, the widow of Wroe Freeman, who was publisher of the *Pine Bluff Commercial* from 1945 to 1974. Mrs. Freeman was a regular around the plant before and after his death. Even during her last, debilitating illness, there was a period when one could look forward to her dropping by, usually on Thursdays after her appointment at the hairdresser's, for a soft drink with the "girls."

When Mrs. Freeman was in the building, you could *tell*. There was the way her voice carried (being deaf, she had no way of determining its volume) and the distinctive sound of those Virginia vowels, which she never lost and never intended to lose.

But most of all, people knew whose presence they were in by the way she would look straight at you to pay a compliment, or leave an encouraging word, or deliver a brief lesson from the life of The Greatest Man This Country Ever Produced, Robert E. Lee. It was like having something of Old Virginia around. Born in Richmond in 1900, she had come to Arkansas as a young bride, but she hadn't left Virginia so much as brought it with her.

We had in common an admiration for Lee. Or as she once told me, "I believe you love General Lee almost as much as I do," which was high praise. I will not vouch for that—it would be boasting—but I am confident that no one could have loved General Lee more than she did.

Mrs. Freeman's ways were not those of this post-modern age, of the Me Generation, or of any other era that neglects the old, direct, assuring formalities. Her visits brought home how assuring formality can be; there was never any doubt about whom she was addressing, what she meant, and whether a response was required. She was not one of your modern mumblers. Yet she was never forward nor awkward, and certainly would not allow anyone else to feel that way in her company.

Once I was so bold as to bring up her handicap and express my admiration at how well—how defiantly, really—she had overcome deafness, which can be the most socially isolating of conditions. When I asked for her secret, Mrs. Freeman looked directly at me and said, as if it were the simplest thing in the world, "Why, you just rise above it." Duty, General Lee said, is the sublimest word in our language.

Somehow Elizabeth Freeman managed to set the social tone for every conversation without dominating it. Visiting her in the hospital a while back, a clergyman and a newspaperman found themselves carrying on a spirited conversation with her, mainly through the medium of written messages in the notebook she kept handy, though she was a practiced lip-reader, too. And when she had drifted off to sleep, her hearing visitors continued to converse with each other—by writing in Mrs. Freeman's notebook. She had set the tone.

What Mrs. Wroe Freeman knew, she *knew*. And what she believed, she *believed*. She loved her family, God, Virginia, and Robert E. Lee, not necessarily in any particular order on any given day. Respecting herself, she respected others. She always looked for that indefinable thing called quality, which she knew was independent of class or status or material wealth. She had the aristocrat's natural sense of democracy.

Elizabeth Freeman was a Lady from a time when that word was not used interchangeably with Woman. At her death at eighty-five, she leaves a legacy of civility *and* candor. Heaven had better be a lot like Virginia; because if it isn't, you can bet that Elizabeth Council Freeman will let them know.

November 11, 1985

11 J. William Fulbright

History Recast

W hat ever became of J. William Fulbright? He is alive and doing well in Washington, where he is engaged in not one but two of the usual post-Senate pastimes. Having passed through that connecting door between the Senate and the tonier Washington law firms, he is reportedly representing Saudi Arabia (at $50,000 a year) and the United Arab Emirates (at $25,000 a year). Mr. Fulbright's second vocation, though perhaps not as lucrative, is surely more creative. It might be called iconography, and the image he wrestles with is his own. Though billed as Deep Thoughts on Foreign Policy, his articles and lectures amount to a fairly transparent defense of the choices he himself made during a long and distinguished career.

J. William's dual role as private counselor and public lecturer suits him. Now out of the political hurlyburly, he no longer need put up with the madding crowd back in Arkansas, or return unwelcome phone calls. But he can remain active in retrospective politics through the memory-lecture, an instrument that allows him to mold the past into ever more accommodating shapes.

A typical example of his iconographer's art appeared in *Foreign Affairs* not long ago. *Foreign Affairs* lacks the light aura of *The New Yorker*, where J. William once published the definitive defense and extension of Henry Wallace's gaga foreign policy. J. William's prose, with its vague air of self-congratulation, fit comfortably between *The New Yorker*'s ads. *Foreign Affairs* is more of a heavily curtained clubroom in which any groans and cries from the outside are muffled by murmurs of Realpolitik. Mr. Fulbright seems at home there, too.

Collectors of Fulbrightiana will relish this latest example in *Foreign Affairs*; his familiar style still settles down on ideas like an English fog on the landscape. He still uses the adjective "discredited" to describe legislation he dislikes, which lends a magisterial air to what might otherwise be a bald and unconvincing narrative. Yet he can be remarkably tactful about obvious mistakes when they are his ("I am not inclined, however, to revive my formulation of 1961 . . .").

He continues to inveigh against dogmatic themes in foreign policy unless they are his own. Human Rights, he warns, can be overdone. Instead, the nation must adhere to The National Interest, a term he leaves undefined except to identify it loosely with his. He worries because "so many of our people and our legislators have deep emotional attachments to other countries which have interests different from ours," but does not worry, apparently, about those whose attachments to other countries are financial.

It is all vintage Fulbright—a bit musty now, but its presumption still amuses. The best parts of a Fulbright piece are still written by Edmund Burke, who is quoted generously. Most welcome are Mr. Fulbright's own animadversions on the trend in mod education to substitute technique for substance, and training for education.

But as J. William views the career he created and pronounces it good, he comes back inevitably to one theme, like the tongue to a loose tooth. That subject is his unheralded role, played for some thirty years and more, as a genteel demagogue on the race issue. It was a role that set the stage for less mannerly Arkansas types like Orval Faubus and Jim Johnson.

There could scarcely be a better illustration than his own racial politics of J. William Fulbright's warning not to confuse technique with substance, and training with education. Or as he puts it in this article, politicians have a tendency to assign a "pre-emptive priority to retaining office."

To justify his politics, Mr. Fulbright quotes a speech he gave in February 1946—an indication of how long this question has been gnawing at him, and he at it:

A sound sense of values, the ability to discriminate between that which is of fundamental importance and that which is only superficial, is an indispensable qualification of a good legislator. As an example of what I mean, let us take the poll tax issue and isolationism. Regardless of how persuasive my colleagues or the national press may be about the evils of the poll tax, I do not see its fundamental importance, and I shall follow the view of the people of my State. . . . On the other hand, regardless of how strongly opposed my constituents may prove to be to the creation of, and participation in, an ever stronger United Nations Organization, I could not follow such a policy in that field unless it becomes clearly hopeless.

It is now only a minor irony of this 1946 speech that the Bill Fulbright who fought isolationism in the thirties, who well understood what it would mean if England went under and the long dark night of barbarism descended on Europe, should have emerged as a champion of isolationism in the 1960s—when only Orientals seemed in danger.

What goes to the heart of his political career in this old speech newly quoted is the choice of priorities it reveals. J. William Fulbright cannot be fairly accused of ignoring human rights only abroad. He opposed not only legislation to remove the poll tax but the whole, decades-long series of civil-rights laws and court decisions that worked a revolutionary transformation in his state and region. The body of law he fought now stands as one of the great advances and redemptions in American history. Yet this signatory of the Southern Manifesto—with all that document implied for the rule of law and of the Constitution of the United States—judged issues like the poll tax of no "fundamental importance" compared to truly significant things like the United Nations, that empty shell.

In 1957, the year of the Little Rock Crisis, when his state was being stampeded by an ambitious demagogue in Little Rock, Senator Fulbright took advantage of the opportunity to take an extended trip abroad. Tracked down in England, he had no comment on the greatest crisis of law and conscience to confront his state in this century. He lay low for a whole month while matters swayed in the balance. When he finally did speak up, it was to give aid and comfort to the mob and, yes, to criticize Dwight Eisenhower for sending the 101st Airborne to Little Rock. A year later, he would file his own personal brief with the Supreme Court of the United States challenging the Eisenhower administration's policy in desegregating the schools of Little Rock.

It's no secret why J. William Fulbright skedaddled when he was most needed: he was afraid of losing his political office. Instead, he lost his political soul. To quote Jim Lester's biography of former governor Sid McMath of Arkansas:

McMath wired and telephoned the senator on several occasions throughout the Little Rock crisis and pleaded with him to issue a statement condemning the extremism of the mob and calling for moderation. McMath also urged the senator to return to Arkansas to appear on television in that context; he believed that this offered an opportunity for Fulbright "to become the unchallenged leader in a new Southern era." To the consternation of McMath and other moderates in Arkansas, Fulbright, who had earlier signed the "Southern Manifesto," which condemned the Brown [desegregation] decision, declined to take any action. He felt his position in the Senate was too important for him to risk involvement. This situation reflected a failure of leadership that was especially demoralizing for the moderates.

J. William Fulbright's elevated abandonment of principle hurt more than Governor Orval Faubus's sheer opportunism. It still does. Senator Fulbright was supposed to know better; he was an educated man. To this day he speaks highly of education as the hope of the world. He roams the globe picking up awards for his justly acclaimed Fulbright Fellowship program. Yet his own rise, which was not always easy to distinguish from his fall, mocks any claim that formal education must necessarily produce moral leadership.

A letter in the Fulbright files captures the sorrowful impact of the senator's decision to side with the segs in those shameful times. A troubled correspondent wrote:

I do not think I can describe to you adequately the sickening shock I felt on the morning I heard the newscast of the Southern Manifesto, and learned that you were one of the signers. . . . When men of your caliber, education, intelligence—nationally and internationally known and respected—issue such statements in disregard of American principles and ideals, to whom can the South turn for responsible and morally sound leadership?

And what did J. William Fulbright do with that all-important position in the Senate for which he had sacrificed his voice when Arkansas needed it most? His abandonment of black Americans in the 1950s and '60s only prefigured his abandonment of Asians in the '70s. Nor did he see leaving Southeast Asia to the Communists as a moral problem. As he put it, "What earthly difference does it make to nomadic tribes or uneducated subsistence farmers, in Vietnam or Cambodia or Laos, whether they have a military dictator, a royal prince, or a socialist commissar in some distant capital that they have never seen and may never even have heard of?" It's not as though these Asian peasants were cultured denizens of, say, the Arkansas Ozarks.

Let it be noted in fairness that J. William Fulbright spoke those awful and all too revealing words before the tide of Boat People demonstrated just how much human beings will risk for a bare chance at freedom—whatever their country, class, or race.

The historical tragedy—well, drawing-room monologue—of James William Fulbright may be condensed to a single irony: Where his influence could have been most beneficial, as on the fundamental question of race, he declined to use it. And where his influence proved only negligible, and now comes to be seen as iniquitous with each wave of Boat People and historical revisionism, he tried to exercise it to the fullest. Perhaps J. William's career might be classed as neither tragedy nor monologue but morality play.

Mr. Fulbright himself has raised the standard by which to judge a legislator's contribution to public life: "A sound sense of values, the ability to discriminate between that which is of fundamental importance and that which is only superficial."

Can it have occurred to him what a cruel and damning standard that is in his case? Yet something seems to drive him back again and again to examine the choices he made. The process may grow tiresome for the rest of us, but it continues to attract him. In a curious way, that may be the most hopeful aspect of his public career: J. William Fulbright seems to understand, however dimly, that he has much to explain.

Adapted from three columns: May 3, 1979, May 13, 1979, and March 29, 1989

12 Cary Grant

Perfecting Himself

C ary Grant's style passed away long before he did; his last movie was made in 1966, twenty years before his death at eighty-two. It was a style that made words like "charming," "debonair," and "urbane" seem not only compliments but awards for enviable achievement.

If there was a single word for Cary Grant, it was not the one overused in his obituaries: "gentleman." Not that he wasn't a gentleman. He was, in the American sense, that is, in the class-conscious, clothes-conscious sense—rather than in the old Southern sense with its antique air of rootedness, family, and inner aristocratic code. And by every report he upheld the gentleman's code in his own outward British-American, trans-Atlantic way.

But the essential adjective for Cary Grant was "elegant." He was elegant not only in the sense that fashion writers use the word but also as scientists and mathematicians use it: Simple. Neat. Precise. Economical. It is not a style much appreciated in today's films. Today's hero is required to be complex, or at least sufficiently inarticulate to seem so; he is more the tortured adolescent than the sophisticated man about town. In Cary Grant's films, the plots (in which he often seemed trapped) might be complex, but he himself was expected to be simple, easy to look at, elegant. He might change character, but he never changed manner. As he once put it: "There was a formula to most of the pictures—you take a fellow who looked fairly well and behaved fairly well and put him in a series of untenable situations. And that was the plot, you see." His character's aim was to maintain self-control; that was the way to win the girl or solve the mystery or prove his worth; today it often seems to be assumed that only when self-control is lost can character be revealed.

"You know what's wrong with you?" Audrey Hepburn asked Grant in *Charade*. "Nothing." The film critic Pauline Kael once wrote of him: "He may not be able to do much, but what he can do no one else has ever done so well. . . . We see ourselves idealized in him. He appeared before us in his radiantly shallow perfection, and that was all we wanted of him. We didn't want depth from him; we asked only that he be handsome and silky and make us laugh."

Critic Kael, like so much of the public, may have overlooked the Cary Grant of *None But the Lonely Heart* and its re-enactment of his bleak English childhood. Perhaps it wasn't that Cary Grant was "not able to do much," but that we weren't prepared to accept all he could do. Just as a great artist shows us our own truths and not his, so his career may show us our limitations and not his.

Nor is comedy "not much" to do. Acting comedy, like writing it, is much harder than it looks—that is, if it is true comedy, not just farce. It requires discipline, the kind that includes restraint, judgment, a certain self-effacement, a talent for timing and teamwork.

Cary Grant's greatest creation was Cary Grant, born Archibald Leach. He was the product of an unhappy marriage, and his mother was committed to a mental hospital when he was nine. He survived a knockabout childhood, grew up in vaudeville, earned his stripes on Broadway, and flunked his first screen test. "Neck too thick, legs too bowed" was the decision—reminiscent of the classic talent scout's report on Fred Astaire: "Can't sing. Can't act. Balding. Dances a little." Cary Grant soon left Archie Leach behind. Role after role, year after year, he worked on developing and refining Cary Grant, on screen and off.

Notable among his acquired traits was that oft-mimicked accent. In his obituary, the *Times* of London couldn't quite place it: "His voice was unique, with an accent attributable to no country or region. It was neither English nor American, nor even mid-Atlantic. Clipped but with some rather extravagant vowel sounds, it went well with the character of a mysterious loner, whose caustic and cynical manner concealed reserves of passion." Someone called it half-Cockney, half-Cambridge, but that is too precise. "It started," he once said, "because I was very conscious of my lack of education and didn't want it to show, so I affected a sort of Oxford accent—and now, of course, it's completely natural to me." He didn't create just on stage and screen. No wonder the director he most admired, and who created just the right niche for the mature Cary Grant, was that master of artifice, Alfred Hitchcock.

Cary Grant achieved the American dream, which has to do not only with getting but with becoming. "I pretended to be somebody I wanted to be, and I finally became that person," he once said. "Or he became me. Or we met at some point. It's a relationship." His was a secular version of being born again, and again, and again. He kept shedding old names, ways, and wives until finally he had molted into the full-fledged Cary Grant.

Cary Grant was the urbane embodiment of modern, anthropocentric man. He was able to depict us not as we are but as we would like to be. And he did so not only with startling accuracy and impressive detail, but also with fine restraint. They called him a perfectionist, and he was. Having perfected his craft long ago, he continued, till the day he died, perfecting himself.

December 4, 1986

13 Sarah Greenberg

'My Fellow Citizens . . .'

Don't confuse me with a TV preacher, but I want to share a blessing with you that I received May 1, 1985, about 11 o'clock in the morning. That's when, happy to accept an invitation from Judge George Howard, Jr., I got to deliver the address to newly naturalized citizens in his courtroom at Little Rock.

Naturalization is a very special occasion—a kind of baptism, wedding, confirmation, commencement, Fourth of July, and Thanksgiving all rolled into one. As an official from the immigration service called out the names of the scores of people who were being naturalized that day, each new citizen would stand and respond with his or her country of origin. Ireland, Vietnam, Thailand, Germany, Chile, Iraq, Iran, Korea, Russia, Jordan, the Philippines, Mexico, India . . . you could almost hear the melting pot still bubbling, and sense America being created anew. Their faces shone. I imagine mine did, too.

These new Americans have a lot to teach those of us whose citizenship is not as bright and fresh as theirs, or as arduously attained. Unlike them, many of us did not choose to be Americans. That distinction was a gift we received through no merit of our own, an act of unearned grace. And as Tom Paine said at a time when there was some doubt about whether there would be an American nation, what we attain too easily, we esteem too lightly.

These new citizens are proof that America is still America, still drawing the hopeful from the ends of the earth in search of the American dream. It was a joy to welcome them as others had welcomed my father and mother when this century was still young. I cherish an old photograph of the passengers aboard the S.S. *Argentina* when it arrived at the port of Boston with a shipload of immigrants February 10, 1921. If you look carefully through the faces, you can find a nineteen-year-old girl—broad Slavic features, pug nose, fair skin, dark hair drawn severely back, unsmiling in the photographic style of the day. A face indistinguishable from those of millions of other Eastern Europeans who flocked to the Golden Land between 1880 and 1920.

That is the face of my mother, Sarah the daughter of Paesach the miller, from outside the village of Mordt in eastern Poland. She was a country girl traveling alone to the New World with not much more than the clothes on her back. But if you look closely at the picture you can see, above the high cheekbones, in the eyes, the treasure she brought with her to this country. Those eyes are full of hope, and determination. If hope failed, determination would remain. And if determination failed, God would not. If she didn't fulfill the American dream, her children would, or her grandchildren, or their children.

My mother's Yiddish was piquant; her English was, well, deliberate; and her silence was most eloquent of all. Whenever she would hear people blithely criticize America, she would give them what my brother, sister, and I called The Look. The message would be unmistakable: What do you know of America who only America know? The same look would freeze on her features when some armchair strategist would speak blithely of war or hunger or poverty in her presence. Having grown up in the midst of the chaos that was the First World War, she did not take such things lightly.

Sometimes, when I examine that old photograph, or when I visit the national cemetery and battlefield at Vicksburg and drive past the still monuments that mark the site of so much bloody confusion and sacrifice and utter determination, or when I read a public-opinion poll that says most Americans consider themselves patriotic but not nearly so many believe they have a duty to do anything for their country, I wonder. I wonder if the determination, the readiness to sacrifice, the faith I see in that old photograph of my mother and her shipmates is still alive, and if my generation could do what she did. Could we put so much behind us, and reach out so far?

Could we hope and struggle so long and so patiently with such moral certainty? I wonder.

And then, in a courtroom in Little Rock, Arkansas, I look at those rows of faces in all their different hues, and hear the Oath of Allegiance taken in a score or more of different accents, and it's clear that the Spirit of Liberty still lives, that America is still America. It is like seeing a varied and splendorous tapestry being endlessly woven.

I don't believe I told these new citizens anything they didn't already know. In fact, I probably didn't need to say anything; I think I could have just gone up to the rostrum and looked at them for the next quarter of an hour, and they would have understood what I wanted to say. We have a special bond, we Americans.

May 5, 1985

14 Andrei Gromyko

The Soviet Vicar

Andrei Gromyko, who was Soviet foreign minister approximately forever, died the other day, if he was ever alive. From the time he entered his country's diplomatic corps and began to rise rapidly because many of his colleagues were being shot, Andrei Gromyko was never known to betray any human feeling. This made him eminently qualified to be the voice of Soviet foreign policy.

Comrade Gromyko was one of the few members of the Politburo who didn't drink—a dangerous if not unnatural sign in a Russian. His complete, almost inhuman sobriety was one of the scariest things about him. The liveliest level he ever reached was sarcasm.

Gromyko the Grim impressed Cyrus Vance, an American secretary of state at some point in the Carter administration-and-debacle, as "a thoroughly professional practitioner of the diplomatic trade." That's diplomatese for being able to spew out whatever one's government orders—true, false, or bizarre. Nikita Khrushchev used to say he could order Gromyko to sit on a block of ice—"he'll stay there and freeze but he won't move." This would do well enough as the job description for what Comrade Gromyko did year after year in the Era of Nyet. (In only a couple of years at the United Nations, he cast the Soviet veto twenty-five times.)

When it came to eradicating any sign of his own personality or will, Andrei Andreyevich Gromyko had no equal. He might have taught old Talleyrand a trick or two when it came to survival, the first being: Efface yourself completely. Diplomats who dealt with

Andrei Gromyko soon learned they were negotiating not with a man but with an instrument.

From Stalin to Gorbachev, Comrade Gromyko curried favor. There was never any danger of his being purged; he was determined to remain ambassador, foreign minister, or Vicar of Bray whatever he had to say or do. ("And this is law, I will maintain, / Unto my dying day, sir, / That whatsoever king shall reign, / I will be Vicar of Bray, sir!") The reward he earned for such canine loyalty was a long and happy life in a totalitarian society, which may be the most damning thing one can say about a political figure in the twentieth century.

Andrei Andreyevich probably reached the high/low point of his thoroughly professional service in 1962, during what may have been the most dangerous confrontation of the Cold War. By October, the United States had compiled a complete photographic record of the Soviet missile bases going up in Fidel Castro's sector of the Soviet empire. And on October 17, Andrei Gromyko looked John F. Kennedy straight in the eye and assured the young president that there were no Soviet missiles in Cuba.

Bobby Kennedy, in his memoir of what came to be known as the Cuban Missile Crisis, recorded the meeting between his brother and the Soviet foreign minister:

> President Kennedy listened astonished, but also with some admiration for the boldness of Gromyko's position. To avoid any misunderstanding, he read aloud his statement of September 4, which pointed out the serious consequences that would arise if the Soviet Union placed missiles or offensive weapons within Cuba. Gromyko assured him this would never be done, that the United States should not be concerned. After touching briefly on other matters, he said goodbye.

Comrade Gromyko brazened it out even in his own memoirs, maintaining that "at no time in our conversation did Kennedy raise the question of the presence of Soviet rockets in Cuba" and that therefore "there was no need for me to say whether there were any there or not."

In the years when the Soviet Union was invading various countries—Hungary, Czechoslovakia, Afghanistan—Comrade

Gromyko would dutifully explain that invasion was a Soviet prerogative. ("The Soviet people are under no obligation to ask for permission to intervene when issues of world peace and the freedom and independence of peoples are involved. That is our right as a world power.") Later, when the party line shifted to non-interference, he would shift with it.

It was Andrei Gromyko who would preside over the Soviet decision to walk out of the arms talks at Geneva. That was after the West decided to deploy medium-range missiles in Western Europe. When the Pershing and cruise missiles had their desired effect and the Soviets decided to negotiate, it was Andrei Gromyko who would meet with Ronald Reagan, and then renew arms negotiations with Secretary of State George Shultz.

Lest we forget, it was Comrade Gromyko who nominated soft-liner Mikhail Gorbachev as the new Soviet Boss. Comrade Gromyko always had an eye for who was coming up in the ranks—and how to ingratiate himself. Perhaps his description of Gorbachev should be kept in mind for future reference: "Comrades, this man has a nice smile, but he has iron teeth." The world will see. Comrade Gromyko is beyond the things of this world now. At this very moment, he is probably sidling up to someone of influence in The Other Place.

July 14, 1989

15 Rudolf Hess

Revenge Is Sour

You don't have to be crazy to be a Nazi, but it helps. See the career of Richard Rudolf Hess, whose rise in the National Socialist German Workers party was almost as meteoric as his fall. The latter occurred when he took it into his muddled head to make a separate peace with the British. The deputy führer, Reich minister without portfolio, member of the Ministerial Council for the Reich and the Secret Cabinet Council, leader of the Nazi party, and second in succession to Hermann Göring, slipped into the cockpit of a fighter plane at Augsburg on May 10, 1941. Eight hundred miles later he parachuted into enemy territory, namely the estate of the Duke of Hamilton, Lord Steward, near Dungavel in Scotland.

When Winston Churchill was told who had dropped in, he thought his caller was playing a joke. (His Majesty's chief minister was watching a Marx Brothers movie at the time.) The distinguished visitor brought generous peace terms, for a Nazi; but after he had delivered a three-hour monologue to his interrogator, it became clear that Rudolf Hess didn't represent his government, his führer, or anyone but his own befuddled self.

Mr. Churchill, who had a way of summing things up, decided the flight was a "frantic deed of lunatic benevolence." Herr Hess was taken away quietly and would spend the remaining forty-six years of his life under lock and key. In August 1987, at the age of 93, he was reported a suicide in Spandau prison. Throughout those years, he never showed any greater hold on reality than he did that curious night in 1941. "I am glad not to be responsible for the way in which Hess has been and is being treated," Sir Winston wrote as long ago as 1950. "He was a medical and not a criminal case."

During the prisoner's lucid intervals—when he wasn't blanking out, losing his memory or maybe just pretending to, chatting with his fellow war criminals, attempting suicide, malingering, or hoarding other prisoners' socks—he would repeat Nazi propaganda. The experts disagreed about his mental state, as experts will, but it didn't require a board-certified psychiatrist to suspect that the deputy führer was more than a few bricks shy of a full load.

One by one the other Nazi leaders sent to Spandau checked out, dead or alive. After Albert Speer and Baldur von Schirach departed at the end of their twenty-year terms in 1967, only one guest was left in the 134-cell prison. The occupant of Cell No. 7 was the sole reason for the rotating hundred-man guard details from four nations—France, Great Britain, the Soviet Union, and the United States. The search lights and towers, the fifteen-foot brick wall and barbed-wire fence, the gates and cellblocks—the whole bizarre routine of that nineteenth-century fortress-prison was maintained for twenty years all for one old man. The debate continues over whether Rudolf Hess was mad, but it would be difficult to argue that the circumstances of his imprisonment were not.

Even the Nuremberg tribunal, scarcely a disinterested body, acquitted Rudolf Hess of crimes against humanity: He had left Germany before their vast and, alas, no longer unimaginable scale was achieved. The Allied powers represented on the tribunal gave Hess a life sentence for the ex post facto crime of "planning [or] waging aggressive war." Albert Speer, who lent the Nazi regime competence and respectability, and would certainly never have done anything so crazy as to go flying off to Scotland to make peace, got twenty years. (Then there was Kurt Waldheim, who, after his real record was finally revealed, was sentenced only to the presidency of Austria.)

The sight of co-signatories to the Nazi-Soviet Pact sitting in judgment at Nuremberg on Rudolf Hess for planning aggressive war should of itself have been sufficient to unsettle even the soundest mind. Yet few seemed to notice the spectacle, and even fewer spoke out. In this country, only Robert A. Taft dared to say that the "trial of the vanquished by the victors cannot be impartial no matter how it is hedged about with forms of justice"—and he was promptly pilloried from coast to coast for pointing out the obvious. It was the Soviets, those heroes of the Katyn massacre, who balked when the other Allies suggested releasing the prisoner of Spandau in his last demented decade.

Those who insisted that Herr Hess needed to be kept in prison till he died would have been closer to the mark if they had cited revenge rather than law as their reason. But the kind of revenge meted out to Rudolf Hess was sour twenty years ago. As George Orwell said in what may be the best essay on the subject ever written: "Revenge is an act which you want to commit when you are powerless and because you are powerless: as soon as the sense of impotence is removed, the desire evaporates also." Or it should.

Even at Rudolf Hess's long awaited death, there were still those who defended the crime that was his punishment. One editorialist went beyond the usual reliance on ex post facto law to say, "Nothing in his record suggests that he would have balked at any task assigned him"—as if it were proper to keep a person caged for forty-six years on the basis not of what he had done but of what he was capable of doing. If that were to be the universal standard, there would not be enough cells on earth to hold the guilty.

Others tried to justify Rudolf Hess's treatment on the grounds of his role in the adoption of the infamous Nuremberg Laws of 1935; they stopped short of suggesting that the other cells at Spandau be filled with any American politicians who had ever supported racist codes.

One of the survivors of Auschwitz, or perhaps it was one of the other death camps, remembered that, when liberation came and the SS men cowered in their barracks, the gray mass of skeletons that were the liberated could have burned them alive. "Instead, we handed them over to the proper authorities," he said. "That was the difference between them and us."

But the treatment of Rudolf Hess blurred that line between Them and Us—between vengeance and law, rage and mercy, nihilism and civilization. Perhaps in death Rudolf Hess can teach the world something he never could in his tortured, wasted, unrepentant, and mercilessly long life: the pointlessness of revenge. As

Flannery O'Connor once pointed out, the proper study of freaks has as its aim to notice not how different they are, but how much the rest of us resemble them.

August 28, 1987

16 Dolores Ibarruri

No Survivors

Dolores Ibarruri was not known by that name when her voice rallied a nation, or what was left of it. They called her La Pasionaria—the Passion Flower—during the Spanish Civil War. And her orations were worth three divisions, at a conservative estimate. It was she who exhorted Spain: "It is better to die standing than live kneeling!" Her battle cry was echoed in every stand of the loyalists: *No pasaran!* They shall not pass!

In the end they did. But La Pasionaria's rhetoric was one reason it took Francisco Franco's troops as long as it did to devour republican Spain. Her fiery oratory also concealed an embarrassing truth: This century's Spanish Civil War soon ceased to be a war between believers in democracy and believers in autocracy, and became the first clash between the two totalitarianisms that would dominate much of this terrible era—Fascism and Communism.

George Orwell's *Homage to Catalonia* was little read at the time, and his description of how the Communists had subverted the struggle was dismissed by true believers when it first appeared. It remains the best and simplest commentary on that insanity. George Orwell fought with the republicans in Spain and, after being wounded by the Fascists, had to flee the country in fear of the Communists. La Pasionaria, however, never wavered. The party afforded her a safe haven in exile, and when a free Spain was at last possible, she returned as Communist as ever, a living relic to the party faithful.

Now she has died there, at the age of 93. Her funeral in Madrid was that of a Marxist saint. It ended with a recording of her imperishable voice and the immense crowd singing the "Internationale." There were delegations from every left-wing cause, but particularly notable were those from the last and most repressive strongholds of the crumbling universe in which she believed to the end—Cuba, the Sandinistas' Nicaragua, and Communist China, each with its own atrocities to display alongside those of the party in Spain half a century ago.

George Marchais, the long-time personification of the French Communist party, said of the guest of honor: "She has contributed to what socialism is today." No doubt he meant it as a tribute, but in December 1989 it sounds like a judgment. The unwavering, unseeing, uncritical zeal that La Pasionaria represented has now led to the collapse from within of one totalitarian regime after another. Across Europe, freedom returns like a long awaited spring.

No survivors were listed in the obituary of Dolores Ibarruri. She was preceded in death by Communism.

December 8, 1989

17 Jesse Jackson

Nullifying the Black Vote

Jesse Jackson's presidential campaign has become a quadrennial American entertainment—as predictable as leap year and as substantial as the Oscars. This show may not do much for Americans black or white, but its star reaps many benefits—not least a virtual immunity from criticism by his rivals, since each would like to win his endorsement when he concedes, as he inevitably will.

Unlike the other losers, the Reverend Mr. Jackson has a ready-made excuse: racial prejudice. Every four years, he buttresses his position as *the* spokesman for black America. No wonder he keeps running. It's the best way to continue his real career—self-promotion. Win or lose, Jesse Jackson wins.

But for black Americans in general, the prospects are not as happy. The black underclass in the country's great cities continues to fester. Riddled by crime, poverty, drugs, and idleness, it passed beyond despair some time ago. Statistics are harrowing whatever the category—unemployment, teenage pregnancies, homicides—and the reality far more so. While Jesse Jackson's presidential campaigns have prospered, black America hasn't.

Maybe there's a connection. The Jackson campaign, by monopolizing the black vote, has rendered it impotent. Why should other presidential candidates compete for that vote if Jesse Jackson has it sewn up? Why should candidates discuss causes close to the black community if campaigning for Brother Jackson has replaced them all, and drained away the energies that might once have gone into pushing a black political agenda?

The Jackson campaign regularly reduces black politics to a campaign chant ("Run, Jesse, Run!") and an empty nostrum or two—like building a fence around America to keep corporations from investing abroad. When a candidate like Dick Gephardt talks like this, it's clear he's being an opportunist and demagogue. When Jesse Jackson does, the David Broders and Mario Cuomos nod sagely and say the party needs to pay attention to his "message." Seldom has the double standard been so clear or so sad. This kind of intellectual condescension is only the reverse side of the same old racial prejudice.

Any notion that Jesse Jackson's appeal goes substantially beyond race was unmasked once again by the results in the 1988 Illinois primary. Campaigning in the state that he had made his home for two decades, he managed to get only 7 percent of the white vote. Despite vigorous efforts, he failed to do well among Hispanic voters in either Texas or Illinois. To quote one analyst on Mr. Jackson's prospects after the results of Super Tuesday were in: "Give him one hundred percent of the black vote and twenty percent of the white vote, twice what he's been getting, and he doesn't come close to carrying a big state." Only in small, tightly organized states, or a few chronically liberal ones, can he hope to broaden his appeal.

Despite his claims, Jesse Jackson is not waging a national campaign; his base may not be geographical, but it is racial—as racial as George Wallace's once was. Can anyone imagine a white candidate who had never held public office or a prominent position in the private economy doing as well as Jesse Jackson did in the 1988 campaign?

The many differences between Jesse Jackson and Martin Luther King, Jr., whose name Mr. Jackson may invoke, are striking. Dr. King was never a political candidate; Jesse Jackson is *only* a political candidate. Dr. King unleashed energies in the black community; Jesse Jackson harnesses those energies to his own political ambition. Dr. King's appeal was above party, even above politics. Jesse Jackson is not only a partisan but one who can put his party's interest below his own. After Democratic hopes were given a decent burial in 1984, Walter Mondale looked back and declared that his endless negotiations with Jesse Jackson that year constituted "the single biggest mistake I made." (He must have forgotten his choice of a running mate.)

Most destructive of all, Jesse Jackson has rendered the black vote meaningless by appropriating it for himself. If that vote were up for grabs, the other Democratic candidates might bid for it strenuously. Instead, the black vote is taken for granted, and the other candidates prepare to bid for the support of its keeper. Even Republicans, once the party of Lincoln, might be more amenable to black interests if the Reverend Mr. Jackson had not set out to make his own election the chief and virtually only black interest visible in national politics.

If Jesse Jackson were not a candidate, both parties might vie to support black causes the way they do to support Israel. Jews, Italians, Southerners, Hispanics, and fifty-seven other varieties of Americans who split their votes find themselves courted by presidential candidates of both parties. But black Americans, by signing over their political proxy to one party and, in the past couple of presidential elections, to one candidate, have effectively disenfranchised themselves. Why should the other presidential candidates bid for a vote that's already cast?

Nathaniel D. Stevens put it this way in the *Lincoln Review*:

Black loyalty to the long-dead "New Deal" and the thankless Democratic Party is . . . a colossal calamity for persons of color in America. It illustrates the danger of being a one-party ethnic group—when your man loses, you are a loser. Your side can't give you anything and the winners come into office not owing you anything. . . . We don't all have to become Republicans again or form a third party, but we do have to put the Black vote up for grabs.

Today one party is certain of the black vote, and the other assumes it won't get it. In a two-party system, that's a recipe for powerlessness. And that's why, when Jesse Jackson wins, black Americans lose.

March 30, 1988

18 Scoop Jackson

Goodbye to the Best

You can tell the way the country is heading by the kind of man it produces, says a character in the novel *Hud*. You can also tell by the kind of man it passes over. That's why the loss of Henry M. Jackson was saddening in more ways than one. He was about the best this country could produce, and he lost two tries for the presidency.

Scoop Jackson's qualities were once considered ordinary in a leader. The man had an elementary decency; honesty came naturally to him. "Mr. Integrity" is what one of his colleagues called him in a eulogy, employing a phrase Everett Dirksen had used to describe another remarkable but not quite fashionable senator, Robert A. Taft. Scoop Jackson had a respect for civil discourse and the rights of others that earned him the praise even of those who fought him. "No one could disagree more vigorously or effectively without being disagreeable than Scoop," remembers Wisconsin's William Proxmire.

Those qualities may explain Senator Jackson's politics, a non-ideological blend that went out of fashion at about the same time a bipartisan foreign policy did. Deeply attached to liberty at home and abroad, he wound up fighting Joe McCarthy before it was usual—and kept on fighting the Cold War after that practice had gone out of fashion. He was still blasting the Soviets the night he died. If his political stands were a rare blend, they were consistent throughout a long, long career. He had an instinctive understanding of tyrannies that often made him a prophet in foreign affairs.

(While flying over Afghanistan in 1954, he looked down on a new road being built from the Soviet border to Kabul and mentioned in his dry way, "Right there is the invasion route that Russia will someday take to Afghanistan.") Just trust the dictatorships to do their worst, and how far wrong can a fellow go in the twentieth century?

The senator from Washington was one of those rare politicians who understand power even if they do not abuse it. No one on the Hill outdid him in looking after the interests of his constituents. He fully earned the sobriquet "Senator from Boeing." In short, he was a linchpin, maybe *the* linchpin, of the nation's military-industrial complex, with all its potential for good or ill. A military-industrial complex being a necessity for the survival of a great power in this age, it was a comfort to have him pulling the levers, and it is unsettling to realize he no longer will be.

His constituents repaid Senator Jackson with a devotion that was no less impressive for being deserved. In 1976, he was re-elected to the Senate with 710,000 votes—the largest number ever cast for any office in the state of Washington. He had served continuously in Congress since 1941, longer than any other senator. He had just cast his 11,000th vote, a characteristic one in favor of a new American nerve-gas program to deter the Soviets from using their extensive chemical arsenal.

Scoop Jackson was no saint and didn't claim to be one; he was a realistic negotiator who knew how to bargain. The Jackson Amendment resulted in the Soviets' letting a quarter of a million people out of their prison-house of a country; many of those people are now living in this country and raising their children in freedom. How many other politicians today could claim so tangible an advance for human liberty? He was equally zealous for civil rights at home, for the rights of labor unions, and for saving the endangered American environment. Politically, he was not bound by any party line. Or as he once put it when refusing to go along with some kneejerk response, "I'm a liberal but not a fool."

Long before his last years, Senator Jackson seemed an old-fashioned type, which is a criticism not of his politics but of the new fashions. Yes, you can tell where a country's headed by the type of leaders it passes over. Many with less character and competence and certainly less integrity made it to the top of the greasy pole while Scoop Jackson was confined to a supporting role. What does it say about the direction of the country that his party should have chosen George McGovern over Scoop Jackson in 1972, and Jimmy Carter over him in 1976? It says nothing assuring.

Let us now carp about famous men. Henry Jackson had a hold on the Jeffersonian spirit, but not the Jeffersonian philosophy—or perhaps any political philosophy. He was a practitioner, not a dreamer, and Americans go to their leaders for dreams, not programs. Scoop Jackson could not give them a new, Jeffersonian vision. He was as boring as the good, decent, and workaday can be.

Scoop Jackson was an expert at the gears and levers of politics, not its essence. He was a craftsman, not an artist. When he won the Pennsylvania primary in the spring of 1976 and had his first and, as it turned out, last chance at national exposure in the presidential sweepstakes, he spent it analyzing the mechanics of his victory, talking about the role of unions and mailing lists and organizers. In one presidential primary in Florida, he stained his reputation by a brief flirtation with busophobia, a still virulent distraction in American politics. He did it for no good reason and to no apparent effect. It may have been the only time he sold his principles short.

This man of competence and decency, of good intentions and the best political instincts, may not have been able to offer eloquence and vision. But he was the best of our time. What does that say about our time?

September 9, 1983

19 George Kennan

The Mirror of History

My eyes widened on seeing the blurb on the front page of the *New York Review of Books*: "George F. Kennan on Arnold Toynbee." Perfect. Inspired. Who better to assay Toynbee than our own chronicler of the decline and fall of the American republic?

Like Toynbee, George Foster Kennan is an icon of the age, a figure more cited and admired than read. He is a fading presence slightly lost in a world he did so much to make. Unlike Toynbee, George Kennan is a working historian and not a para-philosopher masquerading as one.

Ambassador Kennan begins his article on Toynbee by supplying a brief, slightly amused description of how Henry Luce made this last of the Victorians an American cultural artifact. It was as if the word went out to the whole Time-Life empire: Puff Toynbee. It did. And it worked. Who has not heard of Toynbee? Thanks to the genius of America (advertising), Arnold Toynbee must be the world's best known if least read historian.

Once the Luce-Toynbee connection is explained, Professor Kennan sinks into an elegiac tact, and commits the kind of prose adopted by book reviewers who want to say something kind around the edges of their knife-sharp criticism. He takes his cue from the magisterial Dutch historian Peter Geyl, who found Toynbee's work a hodgepodge of error, pretension, and sheer prejudice but tried to be nice about it. The Dutchman was a master of the equivocal praise that rises to high art when practiced by university presidents conferring honorary degrees on big givers, or ministers presiding over funerals for the slightly tarnished.

Here is a sample of Geyl on Toynbee as selected by Kennan: "The reading, the learning, are almost without precedent. Toynbee moves confidently. . . . [His] is a remarkable mind, unusual in our everyday world of historians." Beautiful. No one could argue with that. Toynbee's history *was* almost unprecedented; one might say it was almost unsupported. Indeed he was different from everyday historians, or from any other kind.

Toynbee's history, which is to history as Disneyland is to Orlando, has been exposed by many a scholar besides Peter Geyl (Pitirim Sorokin, Herbert Muller, José Ortega y Gasset) and exploded in one of the most delightful critiques of pseudo-scholarship ever penned, *The Professor and the Fossil* by Maurice Samuel. If James Thurber had been an intellectual, he would have written like Mr. Samuel, to wit: "Professor Sorokin makes it appear that it is necessary to have read his formidable *Social and Cultural Dynamics* in order to see that Professor Toynbee is all wrong. This is a mistake. The irrefutable proof that Professor Toynbee is wrong is supplied by Professor Toynbee himself, who invalidates his own thesis without the assistance of other historians."

Arnold Toynbee was the pointillist of modern historians, producing theses that reflect reality only if one does not examine them up close, whereupon they dissolve into splotchy dots. Peter Geyl again: "There is hardly an incident or a phenomenon quoted by Toynbee to illustrate a particular thesis that does not give rise to qualifications in the reader's mind." One reason for the widespread esteem in which Toynbee is still held is that he specialized in obscure eras. The less one knows about an era, the more persuasive Toynbee's rendering of it.

George Kennan's appraisal of Toynbee was delivered on the occasion of his receiving the Toynbee Prize for 1988–89; his graceful acceptance demonstrates that he remains a diplomat, since the honor is the equivalent of a geneticist's receiving the Lysenko Award. George Kennan is too much the gentleman to be blunt, but too much the historian to ignore the un-ignorable problems of Toynbeean history: the emotional flatness; the tendency to submit all data to the historian's own Procrustean theories; the inability to identify with the individual in history or perhaps even with individual nations; and the imperviousness to the role of sheer luck—good, bad, or indifferent—in human events. That will do for starters. As for an end, George Kennan used Peter Geyl's verdict on Toynbee's work: "It's magnificent, but it's not history!"

It occurs to a longtime Kennan watcher that in a way the professor was delivering a self-critique, for his own theories/complaints about the conduct of American affairs also display a sad impersonality, a studied alienation from the emotional essence of his subject, a tone-deafness to things American, and, yes, an imperviousness to the unaccountable in history. Call it luck or fortuitousness or destiny. Nothing could be further from the spirit, or spiritlessness, of Kennanism than the mystical theory that Providence looks after fools, drunkards, and the United States of America.

There is a school of diplomatic history that thinks of America as solely a geographical rather than a psychological designation, a great power rather than a great idea. Call it the School of Unrealistic Realpolitik, and George F. Kennan is its dean. Crippled by their own ineffable snobbism, its leading lights are regularly confounded, and not a little irritated, by the perennial rebirth of American society and American ideas. Here is a country, an idea, that refuses to abide by the Toynbeean rules or any others. And there is no clear explanation for this phenomenon that does not outrage their refined sensibilities.

The conferring of the Toynbee Prize on George Kennan is an invitation to ironic reflection, but it is scarcely the first irony in his career. Ambassador Kennan has been the most persistent apostle of appeasement in the American diplomatic corps since Munich, yet he won a place in popular history as the strategist whose policy of containment won the Cold War for the West. (He has never forgiven Harry Truman for putting teeth in his policy and so setting the pattern for victory.)

The ironies abound. George Kennan's obsession with the national interest in foreign policy has estranged him from the national character that should inform that interest, no matter how hard the apostles of Realpolitik might like to separate the two. Two decades ago, Mr. Kennan described with characteristic eloquence how the professional diplomat ceases to understand his own country as he comes to understand others. He himself has proven the most poignant example of that process. The ironic result: Even as he planned the strategy that would preserve American values, he lost contact with those values.

The unique character of the American experiment has been lost on George Kennan. The theory, or rather faith, of American exceptionalism makes no more sense to him than it would to Arnold Toynbee, who clearly resented any people so perverse as to violate his rules and refuse to decline on schedule.

It is impossible not to think of George Kennan as our own contemporary Henry Adams, nostalgic for a lost and perhaps imagined past, resentful of the burgeoning future, and capable of the most eloquent misreadings of the present. Professor Kennan was more than gracious to Arnold Toynbee in his address. Let us hope the future will be as kind to George Kennan, for there is something unutterably sad about so much devotion being so deaf to the values it served.

May 26, 1989

Statistical Scarespeak

E ver hear of Coin Harvey? He was quite famous in turn-of-the-century America, particularly out West. His full name was William Hope Harvey; "Coin" came from one of the most popular pamphlets in American history, *Coin's Financial School*. That primer of the Free Silver movement made him a national figure, must have sold a million copies, and had as great an effect upon impressionable readers as William Jennings Bryan's "Cross of Gold" speech did on the Democratic National Convention of 1896. Coin Harvey was the Tom Paine of the Free Silver movement, and when that movement faded with Bryan, he spent much of the rest of his life raising good money by predicting disasters, notably the imminent fall of Western civilization.

In 1900 Mr. Harvey began work on an ambitious, not to say grandiose, fortress-resort in the Ozarks near Rogers, Arkansas, which he called Monte Ne under the impression that it meant Mountain of Waters in Spanish. By 1920, his plans called for a great pyramid there that would house his works so that future archaeologists, guided to it by an inscription on the very top, could dig below to discover the reasons for the collapse of this civilization. Monte Ne was eventually wiped out, all right, but not in any apocalyptic disaster. It was flooded by the Army Corps of Engineers in order to create a recreational lake. Once again a prophet of doom had been defeated by this country's incorrigible progress.

The saga of Coin Harvey came to mind as I sat in the Grand Ballroom of the Hotel Antlers in Colorado Springs listening to

Richard Lamm, the popular governor of Colorado, deliver his standard The-End-Is-Near presentation to an audience of well-fed editorial writers gathered for our national convention. Of course, some things have changed in the disaster line since Coin Harvey's day; for example, Governor Lamm uses a slide projector. But the polemical technique is much the same: Take the most dismal trends at any given period of American history and extend them indefinitely, as if history were bound to move in a straight line rather than being given to cycles and swings of the pendulum. And make the presentation good theater. Coin Harvey had his fictional young hero—Coin—show up some of the most eminent financiers and politicians of the time in a series of imaginary debates. Governor Lamm asks his audience to imagine that he is "a noted historian on the decline and fall of civilizations" lecturing in the year 2050 on the collapse of the American system.

Governor Lamm, now in the persona of a historian seventy years from now in the People's Republic of North America, proceeds to flash a bewildering, disheartening series of statistics on the screen. *"Though these figures are now seventy years old, they are extremely important because they show that the warning signals of an empire in liquidation were flashing all around, but few did anything to retard the unraveling of this once marvelous civilization."* Coin Harvey couldn't have put it more dramatically.

The impact of Governor Lamm's statistics lies mainly in their sheer number. Even if you suspect a single trend line, or know enough about one particular part of the economy to doubt that disaster is at hand, the volume of ominous indices offered by this imaginary historian may seem overwhelming evidence that the sky is falling. For example:

"As you may know, America's productivity had fallen dramatically; there was a definite long-term and sustained drop." It helps that the governor ends this chart on productivity rates in 1981, before the figures began to climb in the eighties.

"From 1963 to 1980, scores on the Scholastic Aptitude Test in the United States dropped dramatically. Verbal scores fell 50 points on a scale of 800; math scores dropped nearly 40 points." Again, the fictive historian prudently ends his study in 1981, before SAT scores began to rise again. The 1985 college entrance exams showed the

greatest improvement in something like twenty-two years. No need
to mention other details, either—like the back-to-basics movement,
and the general emphasis on higher standards in the schools.

*"America the exporter turned into America the importer. For 100
years, from 1870 to 1970, America exported tremendous amounts of
goods, ran up substantial trade surpluses, and generally built a phenom-
enal stock of wealth. Then America began to import far more than it
exported. By 1984, the trade deficit was $130 billion. . . . In 1985 it
became a debtor nation."* It helps to forget the first 100 years of the
republic's history as a debtor nation, when the basis for its later
progress was laid. Above all, don't wonder why so many foreign
exporters are willing to exchange their goods for the American
dollar.

And so dismally on: *The national debt is ruinous. Why, just look at
the size of the interest payments alone.* But don't notice how many
Americans are collecting the interest, and how many foreigners are
reinvesting theirs in this country, where they feel their money is
safest.

*The country is about to be swamped by a tidal wave of the tired, poor,
and hungry. Illegal immigrants are pouring across the borders.* Don't
think about what it is that still attracts people from all over the
world to the Golden Door. Ignore the studies indicating that
immigrants, legal or illegal, are proving an economic boon.

There is nothing like fatuous exaggeration to make one feel
better about problems, however real they are. Listening to Richard
Lamm, I am beset by a wave of optimism. His appraisal is so
disproportionate that it . . . restores proportion. Governor Lamm
and his magic lantern ought to be dispatched to any parts of the
country feeling particularly down. His presentation can be summed
up in the words of the Austrian general who described his position
on the battlefield as "desperate but not serious."

This remarkable effect is achieved mainly by a simple omission,
that of historical perspective. How serious about history can anybody be who quotes Toynbee in his opening paragraph? Another
sign of the less-than-serious is the use of the telltale phrase, "History shows. . . ." Politicians use such language, not historians. The
latter know that history shows just about anything historians want
it to. The one quotation of the evening that is most apt comes from

Schopenhauer: "Every person confuses the limits of his mind with the limits of his world."

This is not to say that Richard Lamm is some kind of hysteric. On the contrary, he would seem to have entirely too much innate sense to believe his own premises, or at least act on them. That's where the analogy with old Coin Harvey breaks down. Governor Lamm isn't planning to build a redoubt in the Ozarks against the coming End of America As We Have Known It. He isn't even running for re-election. Faced with The Impending Collapse of Our Society, he's planning to take a sabbatical so he can spend more time with his family.

At one point the governor compares his apocalyptic vision with that of George Orwell. That slides over some obvious differences between the two. The most obvious may be their use of language. Orwell advocated clear, simple language to cut through the official slogans of one's time; Governor Lamm's speech is so full of hi-tech clichés it sounds like a computer magazine. Orwell used the simplest evidence of the senses to cut through abstractions; Governor Lamm asks his audience to ignore all the evidence around them and trust in his statistical scarespeak.

As a governor, Richard Lamm has been hailed as a great success, perhaps rightly. But as a towering Jeremiah, he doesn't make it. He's more a very human Jonah, smarting and not a little disgusted with the people of Nineveh for proceeding to save themselves. That can be mighty tough on a prophet.

October 8, 1985

21 Robert E. Lee

The Marble Man

The Spanish philosopher José Ortega y Gasset wrote an essay about Goethe, or maybe against Goethe, in which he argued that the tragedy of that greatly admired and little read German author was that he created from literature rather than from his life. It was Ortega's theory that "life is, in itself and forever, shipwreck. To be shipwrecked is not to drown. The poor human being, feeling himself sinking into the abyss, moves his arms to keep afloat. This movement of the arms, which is his reaction against his own destruction, is culture—a swimming stroke. When culture is no more than this, it fulfills its function, and the human being rises above his own abyss."

It is when culture becomes something more, when it grows practiced and abstract and perhaps is confused with life itself, the Spanish philosopher argued, that man comes to feel himself safe and loses the feeling of shipwreck—and also contact with reality. For the swimmer's stroke has become all. Its purpose, its direction, its effect . . . all that goes ignored. First questions are no longer asked; the culture is accepted unquestioningly.

There are few better examples of the formal culture Ortega questioned than the place long since reserved for Robert E. Lee in the history of the South. Not the most popular general after The War, he would later emerge as the dominant figure, the towering hero, the embodiment of Southern chivalry. As the passage of time created the past, Robert Edward Lee would become simply *Lee*—immaculate, seamless, serene.

70

Having given up the search for flaws or even explanations, Southerners and now Americans in general uncover his alabaster figure once a year and gaze at it adoringly before carefully putting it away for next year. Lee has become the marble man, immune to criticism or even curiosity. On the concluding page of his monumental biography of Lee, Douglas Freeman called him "the Southern Arthur." Man had passed into myth, into culture, into abstraction. Like Goethe.

On the centennial of Goethe's death, Ortega was invited to write a tribute to the Great Man. Instead, he wrote a challenge to Goethe's admirers. "There is only one way left to save a classic," he admonished them, and that is

> to give up revering him and use him for our own salvation—that is, to lay aside his classicism, to bring him close to us, to make him contemporary, to set his pulse going again with an injection of blood from our own veins, whose ingredients are *our* passions . . . and *our* problems. . . . Let us try to resurrect our classic by immersing him in life once more.

Robert E. Lee lived amidst war and chaos and the destruction of his fondest hopes, and knew it. He had seen it coming. "Secession is nothing but revolution," Lieutenant Colonel Lee had written his son. And yet, as the whole structure of his life and career and country came crashing down around him, he chose his place with the South with forethought, perhaps even with foreknowledge. He shared neither the ideology nor the enthusiasm of the New Confederacy: "I see only that a fearful calamity is upon us. There is no sacrifice I am not ready to make for the preservation of the Union save that of honor. If a disruption takes place, I shall go back in sorrow to my people and share the misery of my native state." In the end, his country was Virginia, and he would stand by her.

And so he would wake each morning and with a kind of wild patience stride into the wreckage of a nation, into shipwreck. With the same audacity and judgment, boldness and serenity with which he faced a succession of failing Federal commanders, he saw the pillars of his South come tumbling down.

Long before the end, Lee would see it coming, and he was as serene in defeat as he had been in victory. The Lee of Seven Days and First Manassas, of Fredricksburg and Chancellorsville—when Jackson was still with him, swiftly carrying out every order, intimation, and shared instinct in the grand design—was also the Lee of Gettysburg and Second Manassas. He was no fatalist, but he was accepting of his fate and his country's. And after Appomattox, his country was the American Union, while others, still embittered, struggled against that conclusion.

Great in victory, he was incomparable in defeat. For Robert E. Lee understood shipwreck, and its temptations of both exhilaration and despair. "It is well that war is so terrible," he said at Fredricksburg after seeing the Federal charge repulsed, "lest we grow too fond of it." At Gettysburg, he would console a weeping general— "All this has been my fault"—and in a stately letter ask to be relieved of command. The request firmly refused, he would go on to the abbatoir of The Wilderness, and Cold Harbor, until there was no more going on.

When it was over, he would let it be over. He said farewell to the Army of Northern Virginia in a final general order with an eloquence born of restraint, and went home. While others were still fighting the war, producing self-justifications in the form of memoirs, Lee was able to close the book. Still moving purposefully through the wreckage, he returned to Virginia to teach the next generation.

Those searching for the key to the mystery within the alabaster figure might begin with his serene words: "Duty is the sublimest word in our language. Do your duty in all things. You cannot do more. You should never wish to do less." Duty led him surely, unerringly across the abyss and to himself. And then it was time to strike the tent.

At the end he was another old man who had fallen on hard times. A defeated general, he was always beings asked to review his campaigns. A would-be historian, he would occasionally ask after records that were no longer available and make fragmentary notes that would never coalesce into the book he halfway thought about writing some day. His grave confidences to strangers would be betrayed and exploited—invariably to his surprise. (He was always taken aback by any breach of decorum, more puzzled than shocked.) The pardon he sought never came.

He became a schoolteacher in his old age, and filled his days correcting the same mistakes, uttering the same admonitions, trying to keep the place up. He had wanted to settle on his own piece of land after the war, somewhere east of the Blue Ridge; he would die a tenant in the house the school let him use. He had taken his fashionable wife and daughters away from the society they were accustomed to adorn, and he watched them wither in a small college town. The only time he reserved for himself was for long horseback rides on his old steed, and whatever his thoughts, he did not share them.

His circumstances were common enough in those days in a defeated country, and yet the last word one would use—the word it would be impossible to use of Robert E. Lee—was *common*. Of Stonewall Jackson, who was with him till Chancellorsville, his comrade and right arm, the poet would write: "The strength of Jackson is a hammered strength, Bearing the tool marks still," but Lee remained "the marble man . . . the head on the Greek coin, the idol-image. . . . Worshipped, uncomprehended and aloof, A figure lost to flesh and blood and bones, Frozen into legend out of life. . . ." Unmarked, perfect, rising above victory or defeat.

But an alabaster hero can be a biographer's puzzle:

> *How to humanize*
> *That solitary gentleness and strength*
> *Hidden behind the deadly oratory*
> *Of twenty thousand Lee Memorial days;*
> *How show, in spite of all the rhetoric,*
> *All the sick honey of the speechifiers,*
> *Proportion, not as something calm congealed*
> *From lack of fire, but ruling such a fire*
> *As only such proportion could contain?*

One of the latest historians to try, Thomas L. Connelly, set out to chip away at the marble and find the man beneath. To quote the preface to his book, *The Marble Man:* "My interpretation of Robert E. Lee is not traditional, for it tries to portray him as a human being"—meaning only a human being. That would be a considerable demotion for the general in Southern mythology, and Professor Connelly went about his work with a zeal that would do credit to any honest debunker. Modern man is embarrassed by greatness and demands an explanation for such conduct.

The professor uses Sigmund Freud and Rollo May and other familiar guides to psychohistory, and most of all the outward circumstances of Robert E. Lee's life—defeat, loneliness, hardship, frustration—to depict "a troubled man, convinced that he had failed as a pre-war career officer, parent, and moral individual." As for The Marble Man: "The Lee Code—duty, self-control and self-denial—has often been described and praised. Overlooked is the fact that the code was an almost mechanical device that suppressed his naturally strong temper and vibrant personality."

The professor did his best, he really did; but gradually, no doubt involuntarily, he began to succumb to the old spell and undermine his own thesis. After a couple of hundred pages, his praise of Lee begins to mount. And in the end the cumulative effect is hard to distinguish from the familiar old adoration:

> Heroes are not made of nothing, and Robert Lee was a man of more substance than many others. . . . He was a superb general, and was regarded as such by many of his contemporaries. They also saw him as a man of lofty character, whose demeanor transcended the pettiness of many other men. Lee did not require a cult of admirers to establish his reputation.

In the end, Thomas L. Connelly begins to sound suspiciously like Stephen Vincent Benet. And there emerges again the familiar Lee, who neither exults nor explains but simply is.

Despite the succession of New Souths and Old Souths and unSouths since Appomattox, despite all the Americanization and falsification, the professional Southerners and pretend Progress, there remains a subterranean continuity in the affairs of these latitudes. It is a serenity that will not yield to clever analysis or scholarly dissection, but must be felt and shared. Complex as it is, it all can be summoned up whole and simple by the mention of a single name: Lee.

Adapted from two columns: January 19, 1983, and January 19, 1990

22 Abraham Lincoln

Unsettling Words

A distinguished visitor was in Pine Bluff, Arkansas, the other day. Arch Lustberg, a communications consultant from Washington, D.C., told those he was advising not what to say but how to say it. Be open-faced and likable, he told members of the Chamber of Commerce at their annual luncheon. "I've learned that likeability wins the job, the promotion . . . the election . . . the acquittal." I couldn't help wondering: what advice would he have given a homespun, awkward office-seeker named Abe Lincoln?

Mr. Lincoln could swap stories with the best of them, at least one-on-one or maybe in a country store, but he was no life of the party, or at least of Mrs. Lincoln's proper parties. Like his stories, this tall, gaunt, homely man was funny only to a point, and then a terrible melancholy seemed to set in. No one would have described his face as "open," at least not after he had encountered slavery and war.

Now Stephen A. Douglas, his old debating rival, the Little Giant—*there* was a man with an open face, sleek and confident, and with every obvious reason to be. *There* was someone who knew how to put a crowd at ease, to put a good face on every moral perplexity, and muddle through—which is just what he proposed to do about slavery, and therefore avoid war.

Mr. Lincoln did not put people at ease. Where others saw peace and progress, he divined danger and injustice. It is not settling to be told a crisis is mounting, or be asked to peer past the smooth

75

surface at the maelstrom below. "A house divided against itself cannot stand," he told his audience in 1858:

I believe this government cannot endure permanently half slave and half free. It will become all one thing, or all the other. Either the opponents of slavery will arrest the spread of it, and place it where the public mind shall rest in the belief that it is in the course of ultimate extinction; or its advocates will push it forward till it shall become alike lawful in all the states, old as well as new, North as well as South.

"It is not Fortune that governs the world," Montesquieu noticed some time ago. "There are general causes, moral and physical, which operate in every monarchy, raise it, maintain it, or overturn it." That goes for every republic or despotism, too. Those forces may be delayed, they may even by some great effort be defeated, but they will not be denied. The greatness of Mr. Lincoln lay in his refusal to deny them, or to pretend they could be evaded by some kind of technical correction or moral compromise.

There are other unsettling words inscribed on the walls of the great memorial where his memory is enshrined, words that it is hard to imagine appearing on the TelePrompTer of some contemporary, open-faced, likeable Stephen A. Douglas. They are words that seem as out of place in mod America as they must have seemed to those who always thought Mr. Lincoln an alarmist. Those words occur in his second inaugural address, in which he views the suffering of war as just retribution against both North and South for the offense of human slavery:

Fondly do we hope, fervently do we pray, that this mighty scourge of war may speedily pass away. Yet if God wills that it continue until all the wealth piled up by the bondsman's two hundred and fifty years of unrequited toil shall be sunk, and until every drop of blood drawn with the lash shall be paid by another drawn with the sword, as was said three thousand years ago, so it must still be said that the judgments of the Lord are true and righteous altogether.

How would a contemporary American audience react to these words? Not by chanting "Four More Years!" Maybe by shouting that morally idiotic shibboleth of our times, "We're Number One!" Or by switching to the sports channel.

Yet there is no record of Abe Lincoln's words being criticized at the time as—favorite criticism of this era—"negative." No distinguished critic asked why the president couldn't have been more "positive" on such an important occasion. As unsophisticated as Americans might have been about certain subjects a century ago, they were pretty savvy about others, like destiny and divine judgment.

There is no more characteristic theory of our age than The End of History, proclaimed in an article in *The National Interest* and discussed widely in the land. The End of History is not so much a theory as a crystallization of the unexamined assumptions of modern, consumerist, be-happy Western society, namely, that the struggle between freedom and slavery is to be "replaced by economic calculation, the endless solving of technical problems, environmental concerns, and the satisfaction of sophisticated consumer demands." Stephen A. Douglas could not have phrased it better. It should not surprise that, when modern diplomatic theorists embrace a theological discipline, the one called eschatology, or the study of end times, it should prove an eschatology without God.

"Fellow citizens," Mr. Lincoln told his countrymen in the midst of that fiery trial, "we cannot escape history. . . . We shall nobly save, or meanly lose, the last, best hope of earth." Today the Union he saved has become the first, best hope of earth. The eyes of newly freed and still captive peoples turn invariably to the West and to this republic for example, advice, and succor. We cannot evade their scrutiny or our responsibility—certainly not by assuming that success will be automatic.

"We must disenthrall ourselves," said Abraham Lincoln, "and then we shall save our country." At this time of hope rather than fear, Mr. Lincoln could have been talking about the world.

February 12, 1990

23 Raymond Loewy

The Shell Is Essential

There was a period when Americans, not Italians or Scandinavians or Japanese, were designing the world. It started some time earlier this century after the ornamentation of Art Nouveau had grown tiresome for reasons now inexplicable to the contemporary mind, starved as it is for ornamentation. Industrial design flirted with functionalism for a while, but it proved, well, too functional.

Into this gap stepped American designers like Walter Dorwin Teague, Norman Bel Geddes, Henry Dreyfus, and, pre-eminently, Raymond Loewy. They created a style that at the time seemed depersonalized and international. In retrospect it appears very American and a personification of the age, or at least of how the age viewed itself: powerful, speedy, full of momentum, uncluttered by second thoughts and doodads. It was an age rushing forward, *M*odern with a capital, italicized *M*, zooming ahead at a sleek, rounded angle. Raymond Loewy's work was the last word at the time (though like styles before it, Loewyism would prove to have been only the latest word), and the word was: Streamlined.

Like many other influential Americans, Raymond Loewy wasn't born one. Raymond Fernand Loewy was born in Paris in 1893, the son of a Viennese journalist and a French woman of drive and determination. Naturally he would have style.

Young Loewy won his first prize for design at the age of fifteen with a model airplane propelled by rubber bands. When the First World War came, he designed his own uniform because he found the government-issue one drab. He arrived in this country in 1929, just in time for the Great Depression, with only an introduction and various mementoes of his wartime service—the Legion of Honor and the *Croix de Guerre* with four citations. That about summed up his capital assets.

As it happened, 1929 was a propitious year for a talented designer with new ideas to arrive in the United States. The old styles were collapsing along with the economy. Manufacturers were eager to revive demand by offering customers new designs, and Raymond Loewy had an abundance of them (with an ego to match). His designs revealed that he could put any product in a shell, paint three stripes on it, and—*Voila!* It was streamlined! But he was much more than a stylist; he was a student of engineering and aerodynamics. Even if the product was stationary, it would look as if it were moving by the time Raymond Loewy got through with it.

His first redesign was that of the Gestetner duplicator, which would remain unchanged for forty years. As his client list grew, the look of America changed, became Loewy-ized. There was his Coldspot refrigerator (with non-rusting aluminum shelves!) for Sears, Roebuck. It won an international prize in 1937. More impressive, it won over hundreds of thousands of American consumers in the hard-hit thirties.

Then came his International Harvester trucks, Frigidaires, and the first all-welded locomotive—for the Pennsylvania Railroad. (He started with the railroad by designing the trash cans in New York's Pennsylvania Station.) Mr. Loewy liked to cite that streamlined locomotive to rebut his critics: "I've been accused of being a shell designer—you start with a machine and enclose it. But in many cases the shell is essential. A locomotive without a shell would be non-functional."

Mr. Loewy's best known and most innovative, perhaps most influential, model was the 1953 Studebaker Starliner—a light, simple, sleek design introduced when other automobiles were about to sprout tail fins in an era of design-as-wretched-excess. "I alienated the automotive industry," Mr. Loewy would recall later, "by saying that cars should be lightweight and compact. In those days they looked like chrome-plated barges." Once again he had proved a trend-setter, this time so far ahead that it took a while for the rest of us to realize it—too long to save Studebaker.

When the Smithsonian put on a retrospective of Raymond Loewy's designs in 1975, the director of its National Collection of Fine Arts looked around at the exhibits and noted: "Much in this exhibition will seem astonishingly familiar. It may come as a surprise that so much with which we have been surrounded has been the product of one man's vision."

By the time of Loewy's death, American design was growing more self-conscious, more organized and bureaucratized, but not more successful. Americans were looking to Germany and Japan for cars, to Scandinavia for furniture, to Italy for typewriters. America might still contend for leadership in designing apparel, but more and more of it was being manufactured abroad.

Where are the new Raymond Loewys? Are today's designers less flamboyant, better integrated into the corporate organizational structure, and so harder to spot? Worrisome thought: Has design itself been demoted in American priorities, lost somewhere in merchandising or engulfed in the bowels of engineering departments? Is that what happens when the supply side of economics is stressed over the need to stimulate demand?

Raymond Loewy's approach to design was simple. As he said after his Coldspot proved a commercial success: "What I had instinctively believed was being proved by hard sales figures. You take two products with the same function, the same quality, and the same price: the better-looking one will outsell the other." Can American industry have forgotten that simple lesson?

July 31, 1986

24 Joe Louis

The Champion

Joe Louis finally laid his burden down, and it was a heavy one. For almost two decades, through hard times and war, change and turmoil, and seventy-one professional bouts, Joe Louis was more than a prizefighter, and he always knew it. He was hope for people who had grown weary of hoping, he was compassion for closed-door and dead-end lives, he was the reason for the secret smile of people who had little to smile about, he was pride and dignity and promise—the real-life proof that things really could get better.

Joe Louis was the undeniable evidence that there were places in this world—even if they were only little squared-off circles—where all that counted was quality. He wasn't a champion just in the ring; he had to champion hope and pride outside it. Maybe that explains his invariable manner, his unchanging bearing. "Louis looks like a champion and carries himself like a champion," wrote A. J. Liebling, a champion of the newspaper game, "and people will continue to call him champion as long as he lives."

Just how heavy Joe Louis's burden was becomes clear when you recall how things were for blacks in America only a short time ago —not just the laws, written and unwritten, but the gritty, everyday, accepted indignities. Joseph Louis Barrow was born in Lafayette, Alabama, in 1914, the year the Wilson administration restored racial segregation to the nation's capital. "I have never seen the colored people so discouraged and bitter," Booker T. Washington wrote that year. After young Joe's first successful fight in 1932, his

81

manager rushed up with a tip: "For God's sake, after you beat a white opponent, don't smile!" He would go on to win sixty-eight of seventy-one fights, fifty-four by knockouts, twelve of those in the first round, and would constantly be introduced as a-credit-to-his-race.

The White Hopes proliferated pointlessly, and so did the failed predictions. For example, that Joe Louis would never to be able to beat Max Schmeling. Mr. Louis demolished that assertion in two minutes, four seconds one June night in 1938 before 70,000 witnesses at Yankee Stadium.

It was a sweet victory and one of the rare occasions when exultation was allowed, since this white opponent was a foreigner. Jimmy Carter once recalled how his family's black neighbors in Georgia would cross the road to listen to the Carters' radio as Joe Louis dispatched another white opponent: "There was no sound from anyone . . . except a polite, 'Thank you, Mister Earl,' offered to my father. Then, our several dozen visitors filed across the dirt road . . . and quietly entered a house about a hundred yards away. . . . At that point, pandemonium broke loose. . . . But all the curious, accepted proprieties of a racially segregated society had been carefully observed."

A quite unexceptional newspaper article of the time would describe Joe Louis as "an ordinary colored boy, slow thinking and emotionless." When the war came, some journalists urged Louis — he was never Mr. Louis—to sign up for the Air Corps because "colored men can see much better at night than whites." He passed through all the ordinary imbecilities of his times unprovoked, declining to recognize them even with a smile. The bums never laid a glove on him.

I remember sitting on the screened porch at 544 Forrest Avenue in Shreveport, Louisiana, and listening to the Louis-Conn match in 1946. The ceiling fan whirled overhead as the firefly-specked Southern evening grew dark and the Philco relayed the blow-by-blow description. I was in my tenth year and was pulling for Billy Conn because he was the underdog and white. Although I was to be disappointed in the outcome, I was not sorry after my man had danced around the ring for seven uneventful rounds. B. W. Smith, the watchmaker in my father's store and a walking compendium of populist savvy, had warned me that might happen. An old semi-pro pitcher, Mister Smith had taught me to watch baseball, to play checkers, and not to make excuses. He may have voted the Dixiecrat ticket in '48, but for B. W. Smith politics stopped where sports began. I never heard him say a cross word about the Nigra Champion. And I never rooted against Joe Louis again.

Joe Louis was a proud symbol. That isn't easy, and to stay one for seventeen years in The Sweet Science would surely be considered impossible if he hadn't done it. Afterward he did not escape his full measure of pathos, when the money was gone and the Internal Revenue Service became his constant companion and partner. He would end up a gladhander at a Las Vegas gambling casino; his body lay in state at Caesar's Palace.

Joe Louis deserved better, because he made it clear that others deserved better. Because he held on to his dignity and lent it to others when every circumstance conspired against him. Because he was graceful and relentless outside the ring, too. Because he was a gentleman. He did not rage, he *fought*. And no matter what the superficial sadnesses of his life may say, he won.

April 17, 1981

25 Mary McCarthy

Author as Artifact

Mary McCarthy was an American institution: the woman of letters. And like many another American institution, she began to grow predictable long before her death at seventy-seven. But even in what would have been old age for others, she held on to enough of her youth to remind one of the clear, even, unshaded light she had been. Her best work, like some of her early essays and *Memories of a Catholic Girlhood*, came early. In that sense, and perhaps only in that sense, she brings to mind Walker Percy, whose later work delights and instructs to the extent it mirrors his earliest, *The Moviegoer*.

What characterized Mary McCarthy's vision was a child's keen sense of justice—transmitted through a thoroughly adult sensibility. The subtlety and depth of her perceptions never upset her familiar, conversational tone. Her writings on architecture—*Venice Observed, The Stones of Florence*—are about much more than architecture, yet they never descend to lecturing. She loved to explain, but she never spoke down to her reader. Her level joy in discovering things for herself was shared with the reader, never forced on him. Her insights were ours. She never *pointed out* anything. She had a freedom from the pretentious that was a marvel in a pretentious era; it went with her eye, which could cut through a person, an issue, or an age like a surgical knife.

To read her was to hear a friend's voice—an opinionated friend, perhaps, but one who had reason to be. Her self-respect gave her a natural respect for those she was talking to; her assured voice

84

simply arose from the printed page. When she was good, usually in her younger years or her memories of them, she was very good, and even when she devolved into an almost predictable leftist matron, she was never horrid. My favorite collection of her essays is *The Humanist in the Bathtub*, which for some reason is not mentioned in the long list of works that prefaces her later books. Did I just imagine that book? Or has the market for the mediocre simply erased any record of it?

Only in her novels did Mary McCarthy's didacticism grow weary, gossipy, and, yes, a little dowdy. Her more popular works, like *The Group*, were the thinnest. She seemed so interested in characters who did not merit her attention. But in her essays and memoirs, she shone. Her reportage retained the amateur's freshness, perhaps because her standards were those of the consumer rather than the dispenser of opinion, which is always refreshing in a writer.

Naturally she would see through Communism the first time it disappointed her—some time around the Moscow show trials. That's when, like George Orwell in Catalonia, she first glimpsed the enormity of the lie. Despite her conventionally advanced views, she could not abide lies—little-white, straight-out, means-justify-ends, only figurative, or any other variety.

That's why she was sued by Lillian Hellman, who cleaved to the party line long after everybody else who was anybody had seen through it. What was it Mary McCarthy said of her? Oh, yes, something about everything Lillian Hellman wrote being a lie, including "and" and "the." So do essentially false standards pervade everything an ideologue says, even the occasional truth.

But how explain as much to some judge learned in the law and, alas, only in the law? One of the great regrets of Miss McCarthy's life was that Lillian Hellman died before their celebrated case came to trial, leaving the courtroom drama unconsummated. Perhaps it's just as well. Although such a confrontation between doyennes would have made good copy, the gap between these two was not legal but moral, aesthetic, personal. It was as wide as that between the true and the false. It is a gap best left to literature, the weapon each should have stayed with in this duel. Now death ends these revels and makes judgment what it ought to be: detached, impersonal, serene, slowly fading into forgetfulness and grace.

It was typical of Mary McCarthy that she should choose the losing side even of the losing side, the Trotskyites rather than the mainstream Stalinists in the battle for what little there was of the Far Left in the United States. She was an American despite herself and her expatriate years. The proof is that she always sided with the underdog. (Naturally she was a Giants fan.) Mary McCarthy remained a writer of the Left, however moderately, and probably couldn't conceive of any other position. That is what deprived her of the moral grandeur of someone who crossed the great political divide—like Whittaker Chambers. She may not have been deep but, ah, she was so deft.

That's all right—Mary McCarthy would have been overdressed in moral grandeur. She was much better at the limited but absolutely clear, sharp, essential, unanswerable criticism. In her time she punctured more moral grandeur than even this bombastic society could produce. As a critic, she ably defended Hannah Arendt when that writer was telling unpalatable truths, and she pooh-poohed contemporary idols like Arthur Miller and J. D. Salinger.

To quote Alfred Kazin, the literary critic, Miss McCarthy possessed an "unerring ability to spot the hidden weakness or inconsistency in any literary effort and every person. To this weakness she instinctively leaped with cries of pleasure—surprised that her victim, as he lay torn and bleeding, did not applaud her perspicacity." Maybe that, too, had something to do with her Catholic girlhood. She was not a tame tiger but, despite her clear-eyed sophistication, a wholly innocent one. Can that explain her fascination with deviousness? She seemed to have so little of it herself.

Let us celebrate Mary McCarthy; the American market is not likely to produce another soon. She may have been a font of unconventional wisdom in her time, but she had fallen to the televization of American culture long ago. These days consumers prefer their opinions like their motel rooms: no surprises. And television supplies opinion just that way—pervasive, undeviating, loud. The merchandisers of American opinion must be under the impression that they are addressing a hard-of-hearing nation. To quote the *Boston Globe*'s irrepressible Marty Nolan on the assembling of the American dialogue: "It's like ordering at McDonald's. I'll have one bleeding-heart, wimpy liberal and three hard-breathing right-wingers to go." Mary McCarthy wouldn't fit in, not on your typical talk-show/shoutfest. First of all, she was literate.

Besides, Miss McCarthy held her own work and life up to the same calm but piercing criticism she applied to others. A couple of years ago, just before publishing her last memoir, *How I Grew*, she was asked for her assessment of herself. Her reply: "Not favorable." It was one of those exceptional times when she was mistaken.

November 6, 1989

26 H. L. Mencken

A Curmudgeon's Diary

Scandalous. Outrageous. Fascinating. Insulting. Personal. In short: Good copy. And just the sort of exposé that H. L. Mencken, the granddaddy of American curmudgeonhood, would lap up and spit out. I'm talking about the newly released *Mencken Diary*, in which the celebrated author, editor, and essayist is revealed as a small-minded hater increasingly removed from the real world—so obsessed is he with his own cherished prejudices and crafty calculations.

The portentous opening sentence of Neil A. Brauer's dispatch in the *Baltimore Evening Sun* represents just the kind of journalese that the Sage of Baltimore would have delighted in taking apart: "BALTIMORE—The reputation of H. L. Mencken, one of the nation's literary and journalistic icons, may be tarnished permanently by publication of his previously secret diary. . . ."

Indeed, Mencken's reputation might be tarnished, such is the confusion between the artist and the man in the Public Mind—if that is not too generous a term for the mentality that assumes a writer is but the sum of his inner prejudices. Only on second and sober thought, if it ever occurs, will the diary be seen as evidence of how a writer conquered his own smallnesses to make a contribution to American literature that still illumines and delights after half a century. The man was not only a great writer but a great editor—even of his inner impulses. That cannot be said of those who let their inner poisons so corrupt their art that, half a century later, the corruption begins to outweigh the art, as in the increas-

88

ingly ignored works of T. S. Eliot, Ezra Pound, Arnold Toynbee, Céline. . . .

Is the lesson of this scandal that no writer should keep a diary? Of course not. Mencken's diary illustrates the amount of mental flotsam a writer of discursive prose must push aside while trying to make sense (or joy or humor or pathos) of his universe. Mencken's reputation as a writer should be burnished, not tarnished, by the publication of his diary. Look at all the vicious little snobberies he overcame in his work and, more impressive, how he used the energy of his furies to drive his prose. The diary may be full of patronizing remarks about Negroes, but H. L. Mencken's last column was devoted to exposing the stupidity of Jim Crow laws that kept blacks off Baltimore's public tennis courts and golf courses.

And doesn't the man deserve some credit for preserving his diary and authorizing its release after what he thought would be a decent interval? It is not every great man who invites the public to a microscopic inspection of his warts.

Why did he eventually let posterity in on his private thoughts? The best explanation is found in a piece entitled "The Author at Work," in which Mencken explains:

> The author, like any other so-called artist, is a man in whom the normal vanity of all men is so vastly exaggerated that he finds it a sheer impossibility to hold it in. His overpowering impulse is to gyrate before his fellow men, flapping his wings and emitting defiant yells. This being forbidden by the police of all civilized countries, he takes it out by putting his yells on paper. Such is the thing called self-expression.

Fifty years later, the not so late Mr. Mencken remains in its throes, scandalizing the country's still bountiful collection of bluenoses.

If his diary reveals Mencken as a misanthropic racist anti-Semite with isolationist tendencies, if he turns out to be as ignorant in important ways as the Bible-thumpers and booboisie he derided, if his omniscience was feigned and his iconoclasm less shocking than routine, none of that will come as a complete surprise to those who long ago saw between his lines. Could anyone have read his essays without noting certain anti-social tendencies?

Take, for example, Mencken's treatment of poor William Jennings

Bryan, his arch-foil, in an obituary "tribute" written the day after Mr. Bryan proved too good for this life. That essay was enough to establish Mencken's absolute contempt for the respectable doctrine of *nil nisi bonum*. Yet, merciless as that obituary was, no serious student of The Great Commoner would skip it. Half a century later, it still reeks with insight as well as venom. Mencken's copy continues to refute the widespread assumption that journalism must be ephemeral.

In a society beset by conformity, and by a respectability not always easily distinguishable from rigor mortis, certain anti-social tendencies, like a writer's, come like a bracing breeze. The Russians long have recognized that a great writer is a second government, but in a tolerant society like ours, where writers are ignored rather than shot, Mencken was a national asset. He woke us up. He was a daily reprieve from what, in his diary, he calls "the however style of writing," which still dominates too many American editorial columns. Why, besides tradition, would a newspaper publish such editorials? What do they *say*?

H. L. Mencken, even now, still says things. They may be shameful, stupid things he would never have said in public—he was, after all, a gentleman. But they reveal the inner dross out of which he made pure gold. May he rest in peace, and never give us a moment of it.

December 11, 1989

27 James Meredith

Forgetting to Remember

There was a time when James Meredith was impossible to ignore. He was the first black to enter Ole Miss after a tragicomedy of errors orchestrated by Ross Barnett and Robert Kennedy. Four years later, he was shot on his March Against Fear. He was always being made a hero and martyr by the stupidities of others.

Now, however, he contributes his own. Last time I saw Mr. Meredith was the fall of '88 right here in Pine Bluff, where he was campaigning for a Republican candidate for Congress whose name now escapes me. (James Meredith is no longer associated with memorable causes.) Mr. Meredith was handing out the kind of literature that's full of capital letters and capital obsessions. It seems he had discovered that the Fourteenth Amendment was some kind of conspiracy to make blacks second-class citizens. That's right: the Fourteenth Amendment, the cornerstone of civil rights, and not just the civil rights of blacks. Some people go through history twice, first as heroes, later as curiosities. James Meredith's experience is nothing new. The man who was once impossible to ignore has now become impossible to take seriously.

His latest pronouncement is that too much has been made of black slavery—that it was "no big deal" compared to current problems. I remember hearing the same line from a white-collar seg years ago when I mentioned the legacy of black slavery. His general reaction could have been summed up as No Big Deal. "We've all been in slavery at one time or another," he said. Really? I asked him when his ancestors had been slaves. He said he wasn't sure exactly, and I could not resist responding: "Pity you people don't keep better historical records."

It is not the memory of slavery that debases but the forgetting of it. Slavery is invited back when it is not invested with meaning, when we can no longer see in our own experience universal lessons —like those of the scriptural passages we recite at the Seder, the ceremonial meal that marks the beginning of Passover: "Remember that you were a slave in the land of Egypt." "When a stranger resides with you in your land, you shall not wrong him. . . . You shall love him as yourself, for you were strangers in the land of Egypt." "You shall not oppress a stranger, for you know the feelings of the stranger." "Always remember that you were slaves in the land of Egypt."

Slavery *is* a big deal when its bitterness can still be tasted, when the sweetness of liberation can still be savored, when the responsibility that goes with freedom is not forgotten but sought. Then slavery and liberation become more than a part of the past. They become History—an ever-occurring Present within, a destiny. "In every generation each person should feel as though he himself had gone forth from Egypt, as it is written: 'And you shall explain to your child on that day, it is because of what the Lord did for me when I, *myself*, went forth from Egypt.' "

For our family Seder we have found no more fit songs than Negro spirituals like "Go Down, Moses"—"Go down, Moses, way down in Egypt land, tell old Pharaoh, let my people go!" Or the anthems of the civil-rights movement when it was still a movement, not a monument. Songs like "Oh, Freedom"—"And before I'd be a slave, I'd be buried in my grave, and go home to my Lord and be free."

It is when we get to the lines of another spiritual—"O Mary, don't you weep, don't you mourn, Pharaoh's army got drownded, O Mary, don't you weep . . ." that we are interrupted, and we remember that it is not fitting—not ever—to rejoice in the sufferings of others. Then it is time to repeat the story from the Talmud: "When the Egyptian armies were drowning in the sea, the Heavenly Hosts broke out in songs of jubilation. God silenced them and said, 'My creatures are perishing, and you sing praises?' "

It is not only wicked Pharaoh whom we remember on this night but his daughter who drew the babe Moses from the water, and the Egyptian midwives who would not slay the newborn sons of the Israelites. And by spilling ten drops of wine from our own cups we recall also the sufferings of the Egyptians. Matters of the spirit, like freedom, know no artificial boundaries like race, nationality, creed, or time. To accept freedom without hallowing it, without remembering its Source and asking its purpose, is to undermine it, to risk making slavery no big deal.

What would happen if Passover lasted a whole month, if it were divorced from its spiritual significance, if it had no accepted ritual, if its lessons were confined to one people, if it weren't designed specifically with the youngest child in mind? Suppose it were little more than a recitation of famous Jews and what they had contributed to the world? Why, it would lack dignity. It would lack the sense of destiny that flows from the proper appreciation of freedom. It would bear an unsettling resemblance to certain aspects of Black History Month, which ought to be half as long and twice as meaningful.

Tonight we go forth from slavery unto freedom. All of us. Come on, James Meredith, get aboard that Freedom Train.

April 9, 1990

28 Martha Mitchell

The Risks of Truth-Telling

In the midst of the small domestic furor that precedes getting the family any place on time, I asked the ten-year-old if she knew who Martha Mitchell was. Pine Bluff's newest landmark, a statue, was due to be unveiled in thirty minutes, and it would be nice if she knew something about its subject.

"A sort of feminist?" she guessed. Sort of, I agreed. Some of the best feminists don't put any particular emphasis on women's rights. Instead, they defend the rights of all—in Martha Mitchell's case, by telling her truth while others all around were lying. We talked about Watergate and how a Pine Bluff girl had blown the whistle on the whole bunch. The ten-year-old said she thought Watergate was "dumb." Worse than dumb, I said; it was wrong.

I realized that we were doing just what that new monument was intended to get people to do—ask who Martha Mitchell was, and what she had done, and pass the message on to the next generation. The inscription on the base is from John 8:32—"Ye shall know the truth and the truth shall make you free." This is great chapter-and-verse country.

Martha Beall Mitchell is an unusual heroine even for these colorful latitudes. I remember the reaction of one respectable businessman four years ago when he learned that the local daily was organizing a fund drive to raise a memorial to her. "You're kidding," he said.

Martha—and it's impossible not to think of her on a first-name basis—wasn't your ordinary, run-of-the-mill, bronze-on-a-granite-pedestal heroine. She was a character, and a local character before she was a national one. Everyone who knew Martha Beall in her formative years knew she would grow up to be vivacious and outspoken. But perhaps only in her last years did many of her old friends and neighbors come to realize that behind that caricature of the aging Southern belle was the indomitable force and *character* of Southern womanhood, a womanhood that will not be denied or dismissed—as Southern men should know best of all, and as the most powerful figures in the land learned in the 1970s.

Martha would speak up, and she would be heard, and eventually vindicated. She never shrank back into the conventional morality (which, as any small-towner knows, can be a lot more conventional than moral). Martha defied the conventions. And for her efforts she was laughed at, patted on the head, and generally dismissed.

For a time. Only for a time. The people she was telling on made the mistake of thinking Martha Mitchell was *only* a character. She was also a fighter and a truth-teller, and indefatigable at both enterprises. It was a matter of satisfaction that while she was still alive, the time came when Richard Nixon and his coterie could no longer laugh off what Martha Mitchell from Pine Bluff, Arkansas, was telling the world in her highly quotable way. Martha's account stood up while the official, nice, "respectable" version of the episode called Watergate came tumbling down.

The frivolous, high-kicking Martha will live on in the scrapbooks and yellowing newspapers—and should; but so should the visage unveiled here Sunday, of a Martha Mitchell with her jaw set, showing some intimate acquaintance with pain and death. There should be no pretense that the way she chose was easy. It was the *right* choice, not the easy one.

There was about Martha Mitchell another quality that is not readily definable. That quality was indicated by the outpouring of support from across the country when it was announced that a drive had begun to memorialize Martha Mitchell in her home town. The small contributions came flooding in, almost always with some personal word of appreciation—and identification with her.

Yes, the appeal of Martha Mitchell had mainly to do with her willingness to speak her truth, and to endure for it. But there was something more, something that seems to appeal in particular to people who might have grown up always being told never to make a scene. Martha Beall Mitchell had the courage to speak up even at the gravest of risks in a small, tightly knit, stratified community— the risk of being conspicuous, or maybe even looking ridiculous. That takes a special kind of courage. It was a quality that struck a chord not only in Pine Bluff, Arkansas, but in all the Pine Bluffs across the land.

June 5, 1981

29 Daniel Patrick Moynihan

*Social Insecurity**

Mr. Hennessey looked confused as he came spinning through the doors of Riley's Royal I.R.A. Vegetable Bar and Grill. "Oh, Misther Riley," he sighed, "I haven't been this mixed up since Mike Gorbachev, that tarrible Bolshevik and inimy of all things good and holy, turned out be the Man iv the Hour and th' savyour iv Western civilie-zation."

"What's made ye thirsthy this time?" inquired Mr. Riley as a matter of only abstract interest, knowing better than to stir for purely credit customers.

"I'm not sure whather to stop workin' to avoid Social Security or retire now while there's still sawmthin' in the pot to see me through the golden-plated years," explained Mr. Hennessey. "I've been listhenin' to th' daybate so long that I agree with everybody: th' onny way out is to cut and raise payroll taxes, keep the Social Security money in the fed'ral budget but not count it, and fish and cut bait. A little celery tonic on the tab might help clarify matters . . ."

"Aisy there, Hinnissy," responded Mr. Riley from his magisterial place behind and somehow above the bar. "Fir a man who's never held a job longer than a week, you seem much consarned about high finance. Don't carry on so; ye remind me of Mrs. Gallagher, who was sure she had kidney failure, lung rot, gallbladder trouble, and athlete's foot when the onny problem was a little over-aged

---

*With apologies to Finley Peter Dunne.

corned beef. All ye've got is a bad case of Social Insecurity; there's a lot of it goin' 'round iv late. Compose yerself, man, and think who's the cause of this commotion. Then ye'll undherstand."

"Herbert Hoover?" guessed a wan Mr. Hennessey, saying the name that always came to him first when he felt overcome by catastrophe or thirst, which were largely interchangeable in his partisan universe.

"Does the name Daniel Patrick Moynihan mean annythin' to you?" asked Mr. Riley.

"Bless th' man," replied his putative customer. "He's th' brave soul who sounded the alarm and rallied the troops and pointed out th' insidyus nature iv the Raypublican plot against all that th' workin' man holds dear."

"What he is," Mr. Riley corrected, "is the senior senator and pixie from the State of New York, who has just thrown th' whole cawnthry into a grand tizzy by proposin' to cut Social Security taxes and stop countin' th' proceeds as part iv the fed'ral take, where it now parforms th' invalyooble function iv obscurin' th' galactic size iv a debt that would stretch from here t'Arcturus if annybody could count it. Just raymember a couple iv things about Brother Moynihan, and you might get a daycent night's sleep instead of worryin' about who's goin' to buy your dhrinks in 2015.

"The first item to keep in mind," he continued, just warming up, "is that, prior to resignin' his post as ambassador to th' United Nations and becomin' a United States senator from th' state iv New York, he looked straight at the sovran American payple and warned that, should he ever resign his post as ambassador to the United Nations and become United States senator from th' state iv New York, he should be accounted as a man of no honor."

"An honest man," said Mr. Hennessey after a thoughtful pause. " 'Tis not ivry politician who'll give ye fair warnin'."

"An' th' second thing to raymember about Brother Moynihan is this," said Mr. Riley, who was as oblivious to irony as if it were a fly circling the free lunch. He reached down under the bar and produced a faded clipping from the *New York Times*. "I've been savin' Exhibit Number Two here since May the 23rd, 1988, knowin' it would come in handy sooner or even sooner. 'Tis as captivatin' an' eloquent a piece iv self-congratulatory rhetoric as anny pollyti-

cian iver wrote, and it's signed Daniel Patrick Moynihan. Listen."
Mr. Riley cleared his throat and dropped his voice an octave to a
senatorial *basso profundo:*

"In brief, in twelve days in January, 1983, a half dozen people
put in place a revenue stream that is just beginning to flow and
that, if we don't blow it, will put the Federal budget back in the
black, pay off privately held debt, jump start the savings rate, and
guarantee the Social Security Trust Funds for a half century or
more."

Mr. Riley paused for effect, then delivered the moral: "That's the
same system, Hinnissy, that he's now denouncin' as a snare and a
delusion and on th' whole less than parfect. I tell ye, Hinnissy,
when Job wished that his inimy had written a book, he couldn't
have known how useful an op-ed piece from th' *New York Times*
could prove on occasion."

"But th' tax *is* unfair," said Mr. Hennessey, unfazed. "A couple iv
schoolteachers married t'each other'll pay more fir social insecurity
than a millionaire payin' what's onny small change to him."

"Raygressive is th' four-bit word ye're lookin' for, Hinnissy.
True, 'tis an unfair tax, but what is Brother Moyhnihan's response
on makin' that amazin' discovery every workin' man learned with
his first paycheck? Not to make it fair but t'collect less iv it fir our
old age—and I won't have it, Hinnissy. I'm fir smitin' the Raypub-
licans hip, thigh, and pocketbook as much as the next man, but not
if it'll cost me the pension I been buyin' all these years, or if it
means Mrs. Riley, the light iv me eyes and burden of me life, won't
get her reward when I go to mine."

"How could a man with a name like Moynihan sink so low?"
asked Mr. Hennessey, genuinely puzzled.

"Fair is fair, Hinnissy. If George Bush can promise th' rich not
to tax their gains, our boy Pat can work th' awther side iv th' gutter.
'Tis a wanderful counthry, Hinnissy, in which a prezydent can
demagogue th' rich, there bein' so many iv 'em. And since a half-lie
is also a half-truth, th' senator has a point. Instead iv countin' the
Social Security money they've borrowed as a debt, Congress is
about to convene . . ."

"Heaven presarve us," said Mr. Hennessey.

". . . and spend Social Security money as though it were profit.

Th' rayformers are right about that bein' wrong. But they're wrong about there not bein' enough left in the pot to take care iv the likes of you when ye retire from doin' nawthin'. Ivry dollar in Social Security the gawvernmint spends, it's promised to pay back. It says so on the bonds."

"I've had payple offer me IOUs, too," said Mr. Hennessey.

"Ah, but we th' sovran paypul know that we've paid in all these years, and nobody short iv th' Grim Reaper'll stop us from collectin' what's ours. No amount of explainin' and accountin' will change *that.*"

Mr. Riley leaned over the bar and lowered his voice to a confidential level. "And that's why," he explained in reverent tones, "Franklin D. Roosevelt had th' workin' man pay his share t'begin with. He undherstood that, once paypul pay in, they won't put up with not bein' paid out. *That's* th' security in Social Security, Hinnissy."

February 9, 1990

30 Lewis Mumford

Old Ideas Made New

Lewis Mumford's ideas were declared dead long before his obituary appeared. He wrote about architecture and cities, and the human values they ought to represent. And while he was highly praised, it was often as a preface to dismissing him as much too good for this mod, mod world. For example: Ada Louise Huxtable, the architecture critic of the *New York Times*, described him as "an unequaled observer of cities and civilizations" preparatory to concluding: "What he never learned was that society did not share his view of the good life of simplicity, self-sufficiency, and community; an attachment to abstinence, higher ideals, and the greater good are not the basic American dream."

Ms. Huxtable's report of the death of Lewis Mumford's ideas may have been greatly exaggerated; she was writing before George Bush's invocation of a kinder, gentler America, and before the general nostalgia for smaller communities and deeper attachments. Lewis Mumford's ideas may have been out of style for most of his writing life, but they persist outside New York and the other megalopolises of American society. His ideas may even be coming into fashion there, though that is no guarantee they will be understood or heeded. Fashion is one thing, commitment another.

Mr. Mumford wrote as if he were delivering a eulogy for the nineteenth century. He railed against the technocrats who were designing a "uniform, all-enveloping superplanetary structure designed for automatic operation," technocrats who prophesied that, with their victory, man would have conquered not only Nature but himself. He yearned for the small New England town, and chose to spend his last years in his old country house in Amenia, New York.

It gives a writer great freedom to believe he is defending ideas that don't have a chance in the real world. There is no need to trim sails, make low compromises, and generally try to make the ideas saleable by distorting them. To defend a seemingly lost cause almost guarantees purity, and in some cases prophecy. One thinks of Whittaker Chambers, who described himself as "leaving the winning side for the losing side" preparatory to writing *Witness*, his great manifesto against Communism.

Lewis Mumford wasn't fighting an ideology so much as an unexamined assumption, namely, that bigger is always better. He was the chief critic of Robert Moses's plans to pave over New York and the universe, and as early as 1943 was writing warnings like this:

> The New York express highways would be admirable if they were related to anything except the desire, on the part of the more prosperous, to get out of New York as fast as possible; actually their function is to increase the planless decentralization of the metropolis and thereby pile up such a load of decaying properties in the center as to hasten the final exodus.

Dismissed as a sorehead at the time, Lewis Mumford is now hailed as a prophet. It becomes increasingly clear that his jeremiads applied far beyond New York—to many of the country's other great cities and to more than a few of its middle-sized and even small ones. Inner-city decay, ringed by circles of increasing wealth, has become a fixture of America's cities and social pathology. So has separation by class and color.

A small town just doesn't have enough people for the residents to go through life associating only with others of their own kind or status. In the Pine Bluffs of this country, we have to know one another, with all our warts, crotchets, and, yes, even virtues and graces. Here the poor can't be shuffled aside quite so easily, or our common responsibility denied.

Lewis Mumford understood as much, and more. He understood that nostalgia was not enough to preserve the human qualities of communities even if they stayed on a human scale. Community requires planning, though not too much. Today even small towns can be atomized by what Mumford decried as The Megamachine. He could be cranky and didactic, but that didn't make him less right.

Lewis Mumford realized that the most important part of any architect's or city planner's drawing may be the smallest—the tiny human figures. Is it only wishful thinking to believe that, by the time of his death, the criticisms he once made of American society were no longer being dismissed, that there is a new appreciation for the simple, basic values that cities should foster rather than destroy?

February 14, 1990

31 Richard M. Nixon

Richard the Third

It had been a fine dinner, and during dessert the distinguished editor leaned back and talked about what a grand job Richard Nixon had done speaking to the American Society of Newspaper Editors. The editor hastened to explain that he had never been a fan of Mr. Nixon's. "But I tell you," he said, "I was impressed!"

"You can afford to be," I responded. "You didn't write editorials endorsing Richard Nixon in two presidential elections." As a member of the small and select group that did, I have special reason to remember Richard Nixon. I cannot forget that he betrayed not only the confidence of the American people but that of my newspaper.

Mr. Nixon did teach me a valuable lesson: that there is no substitute for character in a president. No other qualities—statesmanship or showmanship, experience or youth, perseverance or imagination, intelligence or knowledge, labor or imagination—can make up for its absence. The danger to the country and the presidency may be only the greater if a chief executive's other qualities are not placed in the service of virtue.

If such an observation is more eighteenth than twentieth century, more classical than contemporary, that does not necessarily make it irrelevant. Marcus Tullius Cicero still has more to teach a republic than Richard Milhous Nixon does.

At another stop on Mr. Nixon's comeback trail, the Economic Club of Detroit, he received a standing ovation and was besieged by autograph hounds. An observer commented: "Richard Nixon is one of a kind." Let us hope so. Even a republic as fortunate as this one may be unable to afford many Richard Nixons.

If there was ever any doubt about H. L. Mencken's dictum that nobody ever went broke underestimating the taste of the American public, it should be removed by the successful self-rehabilitation of the Newest Nixon. His return from obscurity is a great tribute not only to his own powers of manipulation but to the brevity of the American memory. How many comebacks has he made now? There was the old Nixon, the new Nixon, and now the third and newest Nixon was being introduced in selected showrooms across the country—such as the Economic Club of Detroit. Whatever changes in the exterior styling of the new model, the savvy consumer will suspect that, underneath, it's still the same old Nixon.

And just what, one wonders, is that? Has anything remained constant in his public life other than the search for public approbation? Is there anything whole, unnegotiable, and consistent in his record from the time The Fighting Quaker entered politics to the moment when he assured us that he was "not a crook" preparatory to accepting a pardon?

There is a familiar aura about the latest comeback of Richard Nixon. Who else excites so distinct a mixture of admiration and aversion in the American psyche? Why, retired crime bosses, of course. The amoral use of power fascinates us. Gangster films, once a minor vice of American moviegoers, have become an art form in the *Godfather* series. The Nixons of the world fascinate, whether they head a government or a mob.

The unstated—and false—premise of such fascination is that a crook, or at least a crook on a sufficiently grand scale, cannot be a shnook, too. Never mind that distinguished statesman Richard Nixon managed to transform a third-rate burglary into a first-rate scandal. No such drab fact is likely to interfere with the belief that the crooked must be clever.

Hence the defense offered by Mr. Nixon's admirers: "Other presidents did the same thing." That no other president had to resign his office in order to avoid impeachment has been reduced to a forgettable technicality. By absolving Richard Nixon of guilt, his pardon left the impression that obstructing justice is pardonable in a president. It isn't—not without the kind of confession and punishment that Mr. Nixon has so artfully dodged.

The Nixon pardon has to be one of the great triumphs of cynicism in American political history. To leave justice undone is to lower the moral tone of all of society. Only after public opinion is desensitized is it possible to accept Richard Nixon as conquering hero, elder statesman, foreign-policy expert, or whatever pose he chooses to strike next.

July 1, 1988

* * *

According to the word from Hackensack, New Jersey, which is where the letter on my desk was postmarked, seats are going fast for the dedication of the Nixon library/reliquary on June 21, 1990, in Yorba Linda, California. The word from Hugh Hewitt, executive director of the Richard Nixon Library and Birthplace Foundation, is that the Grand Ballroom of the Century Plaza in Los Angeles has been reserved that night for the "Dinner of the Century." Only 1,600 seats will be available.

When a personage passes from mere fame to notoriety, at least in America, the result is a peculiar magnetism. Wouldn't you rather have had a bologna-and-cheese sandwich with Shoeless Joe Jackson than have dined at Delmonico's with Kenesaw Mountain Landis? Righteousness can be a bit of an ordeal, at least for the witness. Doesn't the atmosphere surrounding gangland figures tend to be more interesting than the company of the pedestrian gumshoes who track them down?

It might be said of Richard Nixon that only after his disgrace did he acquire the charisma he had always sought. There is now an almost electric current to his same old platitudes. The voyeurish interest in his current appearances never attended his announcing price controls or Captive Nations Week. Political commentators and other aficionados of the vaguely sordid follow the progress of his rehabilitation with avid attention. They should. The process of the disgraced rejoining public life is so ill defined in this relatively unceremonious society that it bears study—if not by political scientists, then by anthropologists.

These things are done better in older, more practiced societies. In Russia and China, for example. There the unperson reappears magically one day and his re-entry is announced by the return of his party card. He is either made prime minister (China) or assigned to the library stacks (Russia). The latter species of the rehabilitated do not grant interviews; they may not even confirm or deny their identity. But they can be seen occasionally—sipping victory gin like Winston Smith in *1984*, or researching memoirs that will never be published, like V. M. Molotov in his last years.

But it is the British who do it best. The officially disgraced has the good taste to make no show of himself, occupying his person in the most drab works available, something in the line of establishing an old-age home for cockatoos and budgies. Then, after a decent interval, he emerges ever so briefly to accept a nod or a loving cup from Her Majesty in grateful acknowledgment of his properly quiescent services to the Crown, etc., and all is forgiven. Remember the details of the rehabilitation of John Profumo? If so, it was not done properly. Like a gentleman's tie, the reacceptance must be eminently forgettable. Surely the formerly disgraced would not celebrate it with a dinner for his 1,600 closest friends.

The redemptive art has not been perfected in this society. One suspects it has something to do with the puritanical streak in the American character. Mr. Nixon's case is particularly touchy. He had the misfortune to be pardoned without going through the usual prerequisites, like trial and punishment. Pardon without atonement is a bit like marriage without intimacy. The formalities may have been observed, but the emotional aura is missing; indeed, it is painfully conspicuous by its absence.

There has been much debate over the years about whether Gerald Ford did the country a service by pardoning Richard Nixon; whatever your opinion on that score, it should be clear to any seeing, feeling observer that Richard Nixon was done a great disservice. Atonement is not so much a condition for pardon as a route to it, and Gerald Ford in his bumbling, insensitive innocence may have forever barred the way for his awkward predecessor. It is as if he had placed another stumbling block in the way of a man who always looked as though he carried his own with him.

How fortunate, how enviable, the conventional assumption runs, are those who are never caught or, if caught, never punished. What could be better than a quick pardon, a clean slate, and retirement to a place of comfort if not honor? Socrates knew better. As he told Polus in a dialogue that is as relevant as the day it was set down,

> he lives worst who commits the greatest crimes and who, being the most unjust of men, succeeds in escaping rebuke or correction or punishment. . . . May not their way of proceeding, my friend, be compared to the conduct of a person who is afflicted with the worst of diseases and yet contrives not to pay the penalty to the physician for his sins against his constitution, and will not be cured, because, like a child, he is afraid of the pain of being burned or cut:—Is not that a parallel case?

To Socrates, to do wrong was only second on the scale of evils; first was to do wrong and go unpunished for it.

None of this may be much comfort just now to the fallen televangelist Jim Bakker, who faces a forty-five-year prison sentence and, even in these permissive times, may actually serve as much as ten years of it. Yet the Reverend Mr. Bakker is in an enviable position compared to Richard Nixon, who cannot earn release by good behavior. The result is that Mr. Nixon is imprisoned wherever he goes, as if surrounded by an aura of shame that cannot be acknowledged. His pardon has turned out to be a life sentence.

Martin Luther King, Jr., often spoke of the redemptive power of unearned suffering, but there is also something to be said for earned suffering: it, too, cleanses and heals and redeems. Brother Bakker may or may not come to see as much. He may emerge from ten years in one of those federal prisons with tennis courts and whirlpool baths all ready to resume his fund-raising career, this time as a professional penitent along the lines of Charles Colson. But, who knows, he could also go on to live a life of goodness in obscurity. The model is the strangely sainted Raskolnikov in Dostoevsky's *Crime and Punishment*, whose response to his guilt was not to take to the lecture circuit.

Meanwhile, Richard Nixon is sentenced to "freedom," and to a date with the Dinner of the Century on the night of June 21, 1990. It is too harsh a punishment.

November 3, 1989

News Imitates Art

I miss Flannery O'Connor, particularly when some item in the news sounds as if she could have written it. This one was out of Marion, North Carolina: "Schoolyard preacher, 10, Suspended Fourth Time," said the headline. "Duffey Strode, wearing a black jacket and carrying a zippered case apparently containing a Bible, spent twenty minutes on the grounds of Eastfield Elementary school, quoting scripture and hurling biblical epithets in a steady rain before Assistant Principal Shirley Ramsey handed out the suspension."

Duffy Strode could have walked right out of *Wise Blood* or *The Violent Bear It Away*. If he had, some critic doubtless would have written that it was too implausible, too grotesque, too much to believe that even in the South a ten-year-old would respond to a request that he come in out of the rain by hurling such imprecations: "Thou shalt not take the name of the Lord thy God in vain. Thou shalt not commit adultery! Men can't keep their eyes off women and women can't keep their eyes off men. Adulterers shall be put to death and their blood shall be upon them! I'd rather get gold and silver up in Heaven than an education down here."

For that matter, all the Strodes mentioned in this news item sound like refugees from an O'Connor short story. There is David Strode, the father, a mechanic who joins the children when they preach from a pickup truck at high school football games. Robin Strode, the mother, says the family came to North Carolina for a rest after winning a lawsuit in Chambersburg, Pennsylvania, where

110

the city fathers tried to stop Mr. Strode from preaching in the streets. The news story has one of those authenticating artifacts that made Flannery O'Connor's work simultaneously real and mysterious. In her fiction, it might be a wooden leg, or a gorilla suit. In this case, it's the Bible in the zippered case.

When the critics described Flannery O'Connor's stories as grotesque, they usually did not mean it kindly. It was she who accepted and defended that description. "In grotesque works," she once explained, "we find that the writer has made alive some experience which we are not accustomed to observe every day, or which the ordinary man may never experience in his ordinary life. We find that connections which we would expect in the customary kind of realism have been ignored, that there are strange skips and gaps which anyone trying to describe manners and customs would certainly not have left." For example: A child appears in a schoolyard and begins preaching in a pouring rain to an assemblage of forty reporters, numerous cameramen, and two satellite dishes. What we have here is the authentic grotesque Southern news story.

But as Miss O'Connor noted, "the characters have an inner coherence, if not always a coherence to their social framework. Their fictional qualities lean away from typical social patterns, toward mystery and the unexpected." A child begins addressing a congregation of mediamen in the language of the King James Bible. The scene is a social and linguistic anachronism. It also portends an administrative headache for the school system and soon enough a legal one in this litigation-swamped society. Yet the story is not without mystery, not without a sense of something old and precious that has been lost and is now found, deformed.

Psychologists doubtless could be found who would diagnose it all in a minute, but to those of us to whom Flannery O'Connor spoke, the grotesque was an assurance. It is another sign that, despite every effort by the spiritually antiseptic New South, the old one still exists somewhere. Miss O'Connor added this final caveat to her praise of the grotesque: "I have found that anything that comes out of the South is going to be called grotesque by the Northern reader, unless it is grotesque, in which case it is going to be called realistic." Erskine Caldwell's stuff, for example.

"The anguish that most of us have observed for some time now,"

Miss O'Connor wrote in 1957, the year of the Little Rock Crisis, "has been caused not by the fact that the South is alienated from the rest of the country, but by the fact that it is not alienated enough, that every day we are getting more and more like the rest of the country, that we are being forced not only out of our many sins, but out of our few virtues."

The great fear of such rarities as Flannery O'Connor at the time was not that the South would be obliged to face its sins and do justice at last, but that it would learn how to ignore its past and do injustice as subtly and legally as the North. It is a fear that has proven all too well founded.

Flannery O'Connor claimed that in these latitudes the conception of the whole man "is still, in the main, theological. . . . I think it is safe to say that while the South is hardly Christ-centered, it is certainly Christ-haunted. The Southerner, who isn't convinced of it, is very much afraid that he may have been formed in the image and likeness of God."

Miss O'Connor was terribly afraid that "in twenty years Southern writers too may be writing about men in gray-flannel suits and may have lost their ability to see that these gentlemen are even greater freaks than what we are writing about now." Sure enough, twenty years later her fear has come all too close to reality in the more denatured realms of Southern literature.

But in news items like this one, the grotesque still lives, and offers a strange kind of hope and mystery. The South is still out there somewhere, maybe not whole or sound, which it never was, but not obvious and superficial and contemporary, either, like one of the smoother models of plastic furniture. Behind the facade of the New South there isn't just an old North. There is still something troubling our spirit, and, however strange the shapes this disquiet takes, it is infinitely better than not being troubled at all.

May 25, 1988

* * *

First comes faith, then the theologians to explain it away. First came Flannery O'Connor, and now the critics arrive. It's always a pleasure to read wrong-headed criticism of a writer you love. It makes you feel as though you belong to an exclusive club, the Royal Order of the One-Eyed. Address: Land of the Blind.

It is, admittedly, a cheap superiority, but it's a satisfying one. Happily, there will always be critics who want to explain the crystal prose of a George Orwell in the most convoluted way, or submit the equivalent of a schematic drawing to make Flannery O'Connor's biblical grotesqueries absolutely clear.

Get a load of the recent crop of O'Connor critics reviewed by Professor Frederick Crews in the *New York Review of Books*. The professor is no slouch at academspeak himself, as when he says Miss O'Connor wasn't much of a novelist and also explains what's wrong with her short stories: They "can all be seen to be performing the same religious maneuver—namely, a humbling of secular egoism to make way for a sudden infusion of God's grace. That is not, one would think, a device with a great deal of literary mileage left in it. . . ." So much for those of us who still find the storylines in the Bible of some interest.

Say this much for Professor Crews: He's as good at pointing out the fatuities of others as he is at uttering his own. He understands that one critic is just trying to substitute psychoanalytic for religious values in Flannery O'Connor's prose, while another is engaged "in a parallel effort to save the author from her announced values." It is the high calling of such critics to do everything to a writer except leave her blessedly alone.

As the professor well says, the critics would do well "to cease evading her intellectual and emotional loyalty to a single value system." But it's just so *embarrassing* to be religious that they can't very well leave the poor lady to her own strange devices.

No wonder only one of the critics, Notre Dame's Ralph C. Wood, seems to recognize Flannery O'Connor's simple message to her menagerie of characters, almost all of whom could be named Jonah. Namely, "that it is futile to hide from an infinitely caring God." Most of us still hope we can brazen it out by looking straight ahead and pretending not to notice, which is the modern equivalent of booking passage to Tarshish. Good luck.

What seems to bother Professor Crews beyond all proportion is that Miss O'Connor was so busy being dutifully surprised by the intervention of the Holy in the lives of her characters that she didn't pay near enough attention to civil rights. (A similar charge is sometimes leveled against Faulkner, who was the Dixie Express to Flannery O'Connor's local.) To the professor's tin ear, Miss O'Connor spoke dismissively when she said in the midst of that remarkably peaceful revolution: "White people and colored people are used to milling around in the South, and this integration only means that they are going to be milling around together in a few more places."

To anyone with some exposure to the Southern vernacular, her words were not only proportionate but prophetic. Anybody who saw racial integration as some kind of millennial solution to the human condition had to be a damned fool, using the adjective in its theological sense. Integration is only a minimal requirement for folks to get to know and possibly begin to do justice to one another. It is not justice itself, let alone love. It is only permission to mill around together.

The other evening a good and charitable friend who had had just enough to drink insisted on recalling the old days and complimenting us at the *Commercial* for helping to ease the transition to racial integration in these latitudes. He kept using the word Courage, which made me squirm. Arguing for integration was the simplest, least complicated thing I for one ever did. It required no particular skill or virtue once the injustice—and impossibility—of racial segregation became clear, which was soon. Doing anything else would have required a struggle. All we were saying in essence, and all we had to say, was that folks should be allowed to mill around in more places.

Her critics seem put out with Flannery O'Connor because politics was only a starting point for her, if that. Her literary power irritates because it does not seem to flow from their more political vision of salvation. That her influence should persist and even grow stronger after her death comes as an insult to narrow sensibilities, and a complete mystery to the more innocent of her critics. Like faith itself. She keeps reminding us that more important than freedom is what we do with it. This is heresy to the well-trained modern mind. We tend to remember the first part of Moses's message to Pharaoh—"Let My people go"—but not the rest, ". . . so that they may serve Me."

Flannery O'Connor saw the belief in political salvation as one more form of human smugness—and she was as hard on smugness as she was on sentimentality. She did not have to be endlessly explaining things; she could reveal and destroy characters instantly in their own words. For example, the woman who thanks Jesus that "He had not made her a nigger or white-trash or ugly." Flannery O'Connor's language had the succinctness of folk wisdom, as in her description of a confidence man with "an honest look that fitted his face like a set of false teeth." You still see quite a few of those.

Some of her critics want so badly to explain Flannery O'Connor that they can't hear her. That is why—to quote the last line of Professor Crews's review—they are still "groping at formulas that might explain, or even explain away, her electrifying power."

May 6, 1990

33 John O'Hara

Exact Renderings

They're picking on my man again. A literary critic writing in the *New York Times Book Review*, Alfred Kazin, has delivered himself of various condescending criticisms of a new biography of John O'Hara—American novelist, drinker, fighter, and nonpareil observer. The criticisms seem directed less against the biography than against its subject.

Strangely enough, Mr. Kazin gets John O'Hara's strengths right —if one edits out the graceless assaults: "O'Hara, as he often told us, had great mimetic gifts and a startling detailed curiosity about every last side of American life . . . painfully exact renderings of American aggressiveness under all circumstances: whether in bedroom or the board room. . . . No American realist described with more obvious excitement the way Americans can flare up at each other. . . . O'Hara's strength and value came from identifying himself so passionately, absolutely, unthinkingly, with American power in the first half of this century. . . . O'Hara's preoccupation was with character as index to class. . . ."

But almost all of this is said in a disapproving context, as though the writer did something disgraceful by describing his times and surroundings honestly instead of apologizing for them. Mr. Kazin cannot refrain from using quotation marks when he describes John O'Hara's strong prose as "strong." He says of the short stories: "There was a sense of menace in them, the brutal old-style American competitiveness." It's not just John O'Hara of whom Mr. Kazin disapproves, but Mr. O'Hara's America.

116

In Alfred Kazin's view, John O'Hara was but a "melodramatist of American social ambition," and "what is amazing about him, as I read him now, is how much demonism without moderating intellect he brought to his special accomplishment. . . ." What does that mean, "moderating intellect"? The ability to stand in one's own light? The discretion to shade the glaring, un-self-conscious light of things American in John O'Hara's prose and in his time?

"O'Hara was not a social novelist in any dynamic sense," the critic decrees; "he was a mesmerized transcriber of people's habits, mannerisms, styles of speech." What does that mean—"social novelist in any dynamic sense"? If John O'Hara did not represent the force and energy of American society in the first half of this century, if his prose was not active—that is, dynamic—in contrast to static and dim, if he was not concerned with change as it affected individual Americans, their class and society, then what American social novelist was dynamic—Henry James? I have never been able to read a book by Mr. James without drifting off to sleep, only to be awakened by a sense of sudden, startling boredom. Is this the model of dynamism our literary critics would impose on the hapless reader?

John O'Hara made too much of sex, Mr. Kazin complains, or at least of talking about sex. Whatever upper-class women did in private, Mr. Kazin informs us, "in their day and age they did not naturally *talk* dirty." How would Mr. Kazin know? If John O'Hara made much of sex, could it have been because his America made much of it? Or is that too obvious a point for a literary critic to apprehend?

What may offend Mr. Kazin even more than John O'Hara is the tendency of American life to duplicate O'Hara's books. "In *Ten North Frederick* the protagonist unaccountably forms the ambition to become President of the United States," Mr. Kazin complains. "There is nothing in his life to justify this—again symbolic ambition, which is a daydream outside any political context." If only Americans had understood that, Wendell Willkie might have been spared the Republican nomination for president in 1940. George Romney wouldn't even have tried for it. And one wonders what Mr. Kazin must think of a Hollywood B-grade actor's deciding to become governor of California and then president of the United

States. This country's genius for vulgarity has a way of making John O'Hara look like a prophet given to understatement.

Here was a writer who had the talent and determination to portray simply a world that the Alfred Kazins find unpleasant and so call unreal. John O'Hara's unpardonable sin in such company is that he described his world—the world of men on the make in a variety of ways—with letter-perfect accuracy, using brand names and slang phrases the way a perfect grammarian uses punctuation. Mr. Kazin finds such descriptions merely stenographic, in the way some find photography mere pictures. But a hundred years from now, if people study The American Century, they will be drawn to John O'Hara as surely as they are to old WPA photographs.

One line of this biography of John O'Hara hits home. It speaks of him as "looking at life without a literary bias, without trying to see patterns where none exist." But seeing such patterns has become the stock in trade of mod literary criticism. Of course a critic looking for non-existent patterns would find it unpleasant to be told endlessly just what people said, how they said it, what clothes they wore, what drinks they ordered, the hotels they frequented. It would be, well, stenographic.

Once again, I miss John O'Hara. And not just because of the job he would do on a literary critic like Mr. Kazin. (In John O'Hara's America no slight went unreckoned, even if it merited only a silent snub.) I miss John O'Hara because American literature just now could use his eye and ear, and his brutal preoccupation with the fact. He could have walked out of one of his own short stories. My favorite story about him concerns the time he got involved in a barroom brawl with two midgets. To borrow W. C. Fields's line about any man who hates dogs and children, anybody who would take on a couple of midgets can't be all bad.

John O'Hara would not resort to forever explaining things when a right cross or a simple line-item description would do well enough. He had enough respect for his reader, and for himself, not to bother with all the tangential junk. He just told the story, as someone you might meet in a dining car would. American publishing could use more O'Haras, who grow rare. The Kazins, alas, seem everywhere.

August 9, 1984

34 George Orwell

The Feel of Life

"Why do you like Orwell so much?" The question comes up over coffee, and for a moment I'm at a loss for words. It's like being asked why you like Mozart, or pumpkin pie, or the color yellow. I hesitate to answer, because the attempt to describe something fine may fail to do it justice, and cheat others who have not discovered it at first hand. "Because he was a fine writer, and he showed how politics affects people's lives." That was the best I could do at that moment.

George Orwell was indeed a fine writer—limpid, honest, insightful—but what does "how politics affects people's lives" mean? Perhaps that he was a social critic rather than a political theorist. He was no abstract analyst; his writing had the feel of life.

Bernard Crick's much acclaimed biography, *George Orwell*, contains a maddening amount of Crick and not nearly enough Orwell. But one is grateful to Professor Crick for bringing back the many reasons Orwell is special:

Because he was a moralist who could reprove another of world rank (Leo Tolstoy) for being monumentally silly, and demonstrate why in a penetrating essay on the language of Shakespeare—and do it without scholarly twaddle.

Because, quite apart from his books that have become classics, like *1984* and *Animal Farm*, his essays retain their freshness. They do more: they improve on rereading.

Because there was nothing of the Great Author about him.

Because the language of this English democrat and Old Etonian had an uncanny ability to capture the sound, smell, and mentality of modern totalitarian society.

Because he was original but never alien. Because he held on to a rare common sense at a time when ideology ruled the political and literary roost.

Because he could see, and explain, the significance of things that the rest of us dismiss as trivia.

Because he was so completely inner-directed.

Because, though he was a professional critic, he had difficulty criticizing anyone he had ever met in person—and overcame it.

Because he had the courage to trust his own instincts, and because they were worthy of trust.

Because he could read and comment on Jonathan Swift, William Shakespeare, and Charles Dickens as if they had just been published. He also contributed a fine study of Henry Miller—who *had* just been published—in the same informal vein.

Because of the enemies he made. Whether on the left or the right, they invariably shared a preference for some party line—of class or politics or academia—over the clear evidence of the senses.

Because he could see through his own socialism. (Professor Crick has some problems coming to terms with that.) And because some of his most serious work, such as his analysis of boys' magazines or purportedly comic postcards, is shot through with self-deprecating humor. George Orwell was a rare specimen—a reforming pamphleteer with a sense of humor and an understanding of the limits of the human condition.

Because he was always a patriot and never a nationalist. He was very British—no, English—in ways that have produced Anglophiles from Hoboken to Timbuktu. He had character, civility, and a talent for understatement. As for those qualities that incite Anglophobia—snobbism, Blimpism, preciousness—he had no use for them.

And finally, because he understood what writing was about. It's still an open question whether Bernard Crick does. Reading Crick on Orwell's prose is a bit like listening to a watchmaker explain Einstein's theories about time. You can hear all those gears meshing as art is rendered in mechanical terms. The most hilarious example of the professor at work comes when he explains how Orwell should have written *1984.* The biographer also passed over one of

the finest essays ever written on the pointlessness of revenge—
George Orwell's "Revenge Is Sour." That's a glaring omission in a
book billed as "The First Complete Biography."

Yet on occasion, the professor catches Orwell's crystal spirit, as
when he apprehends what a fine piece of reportage *Homage to
Catalonia* is, and the natural, understated heroism that produced it
during the Spanish Civil War.

This biography's curious mixture—tin-eared didacticism with
sudden flashes of insight—is perhaps illustrated best on the last
page, where Professor Crick contributes this perfect example of
essentially meaningless punditspeak: "In striving to keep a deliberate balance between public and private values, between creative
work and necessary labor, between politics and culture, Orwell's
life and his writings should both guide and cheer us." And then the
professor can follow up with a sentence that is full of traction and
comes close to summing up Orwell's appeal: "He hated the power
hungry, exercised intelligence and independence, taught us again
to use our language with beauty and clarity, sought for and
practiced fraternity, and had faith in the decency, tolerance, and
humanity of the common man."

June 9, 1982

35 Walker Percy

With Deepest Sympathy

MR. JOHN BICKERSON BOLLING
GENTILLY, LOUISIANA

Dear Binx,

How are you, fella? Are you still squiring Linda about on the Coast road to Pass Christian, or is it Sharon Kincaid now? Please give my best to Cousin Kate; I hope she is better. Do you still have the red MG? I trust Feliciana Parish is still there.

I feel I've known you ever since Walker Percy had you narrate *The Moviegoer*. I'm sorry I haven't written before, but, honest, I just heard the news. Can you believe it took this long for word to get to Arkansas? A friend and I were walking into the Sno-White Cafe here in Pine Bluff when he stopped in front of the door and told me. I kept walking, I even managed to order a cheeseburger uptown—that's with tomato, lettuce, and mayonnaise—but I was stunned.

I knew Walker Percy was sick—didn't he resign from the LSU board of trustees or some such a while back for reasons of health? But you're never prepared, never, for something like that. You hear about it and you realize the minute hand of your own life has slipped forward, and, though nothing has changed outwardly, everything's different inwardly. The scenery shrivels and the colors fade; it's not the same without him to see it.

I have to tell you I was hurt nobody told me any sooner. Up here in Arkansas we commemorate the death of modernist playwrights

122

and minor governors and such, but there was nary a mention of Walker Percy that I saw, and his obituary in the *Times* must have been in one of those that stack up before I can get to them. I felt like a poor relation, the kind of ne'er-do-well you send a wedding invitation on the day of the ceremony—so you'll be sure he won't show up and embarrass everybody.

It's not the same, mourning—or celebrating—out of sync with everybody else. It's a kind of chronological alienation. It lends perspective, all right, which is just what the modern world has too much of now. You can't take it as hard as you want to, seeing how it's a week past. Yet it's news to you. You don't know how to behave, except in the most polite, acceptable way. Me, I thought about you, Binx, and the movies you were always taking in.

It got me to thinking about what you used to call the Malaise, which was a good word before Jimmy Carter ruined it, and a lot better than the literary equivalent, anomie. Malaise was just the right word in 1961, when *The Moviegoer* was first published. Now the politicians have absconded with it.

Malaise: I remember how you described it that evening in Gentilly, when the buildings were low against the sky and deserted at the end of the day, and the occasional gas station attendants were hosing down the concrete under their "glowing discs and shells and stars." You saw the beauty and transience and ordinariness of it, and the emptiness of our distractions:

> On the way home, I stop off at the Tivoli. It is a Jane Powell picture and I have no intention of seeing it. However, Mr. Kinsella, the manager, sees me and actually pulls me in by the coatsleeve for a sample look. He says it is a real pleaser and he means it. There go Jane and some fellow walking arm in arm down the street in a high, wide and handsome style and doing a wake up and sing number. The doorman, the cop on the corner, the taxi driver, each sunk in his own private misery, smile and begin to tap their feet. I am hardly ever depressed by a movie and Jane Powell is a very nice-looking girl, but the despair of it is enough to leave you gone in the stomach.

God, isn't that the truth? What you wanted, Binx, what we want, is some relief from the Malaise, and recognizing it is the first step.

Walker Percy didn't just name it, the way some textbook on Existentialism 101 would, complete with index, genealogy, and required reading; he made blank art of it, as close and as distant as New Orleens Land of Dreems. Reading *The Moviegoer* made me want to drive down to Metairie *right now* just to see what wasn't there, till I snapped to and realized I might as well stay where I was, 'cause it wasn't here, either.

In Walker Percy, our generation at last had our counterpoint to Faulkner. The Dixie Express, Flannery O'Connor called Faulkner. And the roar and rumble of him was so great and thick and all-encompassing when he went by that nothing but it existed, and we just can't live immersed in all that all the time. Besides, everything was changing, as it always does, and who would record this different South, or even non-South?

Damn it, Faulkner has become part of the Malaise, too. He has become the great backdrop against which those who come after have to carry on, play our parts, recite our lines, live our scripted lives long after the whole theater has crumbled around us. A great artist is a great inner tyrant; he can't help but dictate. Some of the devotees read through the Faulknerian canon every year, the way some churches go through the Bible. Is it possible to do that and lead one's own life? Isn't it mesmerizing and exhausting enough just to read *Light in August* every December, in time for Christmas? To study Scripture, a wise rabbi once told me, one has to know how to do two things: to enter and to emerge. The entering is the easy part, the irresistible part. But how emerge? And what is left when one does? A sense of loss. The Malaise.

Faulkner crystallized that sense of loss forever in his world squeezed into a sentence, his inexhaustible world carved in interminable sentences, and so deprived us of our own sense of loss. But Walker Percy emerged out of Mississippi (of course) and restored it to us—a whole different sense of loss, ineffable and inexplicable but unmistakable. A *felt* emptiness. In our rapture with *The Moviegoer*, we were reduced to talking in italicized prose—like one of Walker Percy's less appealing characters. Our enthusiasm knew no boundaries or articulation. We loved you, Binx, as surely as we loved, or hated, or despaired of ourselves. You had that wonderful, almost unaware sense of *vacancy* that still waits for us at every turn.

The specific character of despair, Kierkegaard said, is precisely this: it is unaware of being despair. Binx, you were perfect. The day Walker Percy created you, he caught all of us.

There were moments, just moments, when you did grow aware, when you beat the Malaise, even if you didn't think you had. For example on page 99 of my edition of *The Moviegoer*:

> For some time now the impression has been growing upon me that everyone is dead. It happens when I speak to people. In the middle of a sentence it will come over me; yes, beyond a doubt, this is death. There is little to do but groan and make an excuse and slip away as quickly as one can. At such times it seems that the conversation is spoken by automatons who have no choice in what they say. I hear myself or someone else saying things like: "In my opinion the Russian people are a great people, but—" or "Yes, what you say about the hypocrisy of the North is unquestionably true. However—" and I think to myself: this is death. Lately it is all I can do to carry on such everyday conversations, because my cheek has developed a tendency to twitch of its own accord. Wednesday as I stood speaking to Eddie Lovell, I felt my eye closing in a broad wink.

Binx, would you believe that in the middle of some board meeting or press conference or lovely occasion, it is sometimes all I can do to resist standing up and saying in a loud voice: *"Do you know all of us are going to die?"* I hold back; I don't want to be thought some kind of fanatic. But my soul thirsts, Binx. I can hear it panting. I keep running across the kind of phrase that caught your attention (". . . hopefully awaiting the gradual convergence of the physical sciences and the social sciences") and that leaves us abandoned on the endless plateau of Malaise. Do you have any idea how many times a day an editorial-page editor sees phrases like that?

I always liked sportswriters, Binx, but used to think of myself as a cut above. How many synonyms can you think of for Win, Lose, or Tie? How many ways to tell the same story, even if the names and stadiums are different? But of late it's hit me, Binx. Political and social commentary are the same game, too. Only the names change. How many synonyms are there for Win, Lose, Tie, and hubris? And for a blessed—I think it's blessed—moment, one becomes aware of the Malaise, which may be the only way to overcome it.

It wasn't the same reading Walker Percy after *The Moviegoer*, though there were flashes in his other books. The desperate questions he raised were so much better than any of his wise answers. The Malaise has all the answers; it's the questions that still rouse us, and return us to life.

Best regards.

May 25, 1990

36 Ayn Rand

Greed Glorified

What was it that attracted so many people so fiercely to Ayn Rand? Could it have been her writing? As a novelist, she ranked somewhere below science fiction's Robert Heinlein and above Harold Gray, who gave Li'l Orphan Annie to a credulous world. Ayn Rand shared certain styles and ideological proclivities with both. Reviewing her second novel/manifesto, Granville Hicks commented that it had "only two moods, the melodramatic and the didactic, and in both it knows no bounds." One speech in *Atlas Shrugged* runs some 35,000 words, and when her publisher at Random House (the long-suffering Bennett Cerf) suggested trimming it, Ayn Rand responded: "Would you cut the Bible?" Her belief in her prose was boundless, too. The result was that her hero, John Galt, turned out to be more than a bit of a bore. It was a characteristic he shared with his creator.

As for her philosophy, it was boundless, too, particularly in its faith in individual greed, which she knew and glorified as individual freedom, accomplishment, conscience, and the new *summum bonum*. Her philosophy could be taken up enthusiastically, angrily, thirstily, in almost every way but seriously. It struck the generality of philosophers the way her books struck the generality of reviewers. Orville Prescott's description of *The Fountainhead*, the first work in the Ayn Rand canon, might apply as well to her ideas: full of "concentrated intellectual passion" and "astonishing twists of superabundant plot," but, "like the work of a contortionist or a human cannonball, it entertains without making good any sound claims to being art." Or philosophy. Objectivism, she called it. Subjectivism would have been as appropriate.

She outraged the liberals, understandably enough, and had the satisfaction of outlasting their domination of American fashion. Yet it was American conservatives she particularly reviled, as one despises the heretic more than the enemy. Despite their salutary belief in the free market, they refused to apply it to everything, holding that some things were priceless. A kind of Taylor Caldwell of economics, Ayn Rand was convinced she had found the Holy Grail in man's acquisitive instincts. When John Galt and his disciples retreat to the wilderness at the end of *Atlas Shrugged,* he raises his hand and makes the sign of the dollar, not the cross. But Ayn Rand was never able to get American conservatives to see the light. It was Whittaker Chambers who, after reading *Atlas Shrugged*, made the most damning of comparisons: "Randian Man," he wrote, "like Marxian Man, is made the center of a godless world." How maddening. Here she had discovered that the Golden Calf represented the true faith after all, yet those who should have seen that most clearly still insisted on following after familiar gods.

Ayn Rand cut herself off from all these idolaters and schismatics and superstitious dunces, categories that came to include the mainstream of American thought and most of the side currents. Yet followers still swarmed around her. At the funeral home where she lay in state next to a six-foot dollar sign, they came to pay tribute. There was Alan Greenspan, chairman of the Council of Economic Advisers under Gerald Ford. Robert M. Bleiberg of *Barron's*. Leaders of the new Libertarian party. (Well, that figures.) Various professors of business management and psychology at places like Vassar and Toronto University. And one Herb Grossman, who teaches math in Yonkers. His tribute evoked Ayn Rand herself. "What appeals to me about her idea of rational selfishness," he said, "is that she was right."

What attracted them all to Ayn Rand? One clue is that many were won over in their youth—perhaps adolescence would be more accurate—and never forgot who had introduced them to the joys of untrammeled individualism. In a world where being liberal and feeling guilty had become largely synonymous, what a relief it must have been to find someone as unabashedly selfish as Ayn Rand.

What conventional morality conspired to teach them was wrong turned out to be right, even saving, in her sight. She washed away the guilt. Some of the comments attributed to her may have been apocryphal—that the Sermon on the Mount was evil, Albert Schweitzer a moral monster, and money the root of all good—but they caught the spirit of her brave old world, and they must have been refreshing to a generation that had been force-fed altruism. In a way, the appeal of Ayn Rand represented a healthy reaction to a literature whose moral boundaries were etched by the New Deal. There had to be more to the life of the mind than that.

George Orwell, in an essay on the politics of Charles Dickens, noted that the English author and champion of the underdog had no program other than "behave decently." Dickens was out to change people, not society, and, as George Orwell commented, "the vagueness of his discontent is the mark of its permanence." Ayn Rand, despite all the hocus-pocus about a program or philosophy, was out to change people, too. The precision of her discontent was the mark of its impermanence. In the end, Ayn Rand had no program other than "behave indecently." And while that shocked some, it liberated others.

Ayn Rand was Social Darwinism making a comeback as an underground movement, a secret hope, a fraternity of individualists. Social Darwinism always was full of gaps, as perhaps the application of any biological theory to society may be. Social Darwinism also was, and remains, arrogant and dangerous. And in its emphasis on the natural superiority of some over others, it carries the seeds of fascism and worse, if anything could be worse. Perhaps that is all Ayn Rand's ideas have in common with the great ideas: they are dangerous. But ideas however dangerous can also be useful. They can awaken young people to the excitement of thought, instill a lifelong respect for intellectual curiosity, and be lots of fun. Ayn Rand's qualified on all those counts.

There is an old story that keeps coming back about a rustic type who was reading Li'l Orphan Annie years ago. (One is continually drawn back to Harold Gray and the comic-strip *Weltanschauung* when discussing Ayn Rand.) At length, the old boy looked up from the paper and commented: "Y'know, I only believe about half of this."

But there is the other half. Ayn Rand presented both halves of her fixation with an appalling sincerity. That's why every society needs one Ayn Rand. But perhaps not more than one.

March 22, 1982

37 Ronald Reagan

The Music Man and His Critics

The *New York Times* decided to have a little fun with Ronald Reagan after one of his of State of the Union addresses. The good gray *Times*'s idea of fun was an extended semi-literary allusion to a musical comedy—Meredith Wilson's masterful *The Music Man*, which invariably conjures up visions of seventy-six trombones and Robert Preston. This time the *Times* cast Ronald Reagan in the leading role and noted how well it fit:

He's a what?

He's a music man and he sells clarinets to the kids in the town with the big trombone and the ratatat drums. . . . And the piccolo the piccolo uniforms too with the shiny gold braid on the coat. . . . The fella sells bands. . . . I don't know how he does it but he lives like a king, and he dallies and he gathers and he lucks and he shines and when the man dances, certainly boys, what else: the piper pays him.

None of the strait-laced matrons in River City could have outdone the *Times* in looking askance at the interloper who promised to inject joy and beauty—music!—into life once again. But the danger in using literary or even semi-literary allusions is that the best of them may be ambiguous. The Music Man—more formally, Professor Harold Hill—wasn't the unalloyed villain of the musical; he was a kind of hero. Granted, there wasn't much substance to his slightly Reaganesque approach to teaching the kids music ("a revolutionary new method called the Think System where you don't bother with the notes"). But he did leave River City a changed place.

The reference to the Music Man would be just as apt if applied to one of the *Times*'s own political heroes, Franklin Delano Roosevelt. Talk about a Music Man! What program besides hope did FDR bring into office with him in the gloomy midst of the Great Depression? He ran on a conventional platform that promised a balanced budget, drastic cuts in government spending, a sound currency, and an international monetary conference—none of which proved the hallmark of the New Deal. He spoke of government regulation of the economy "only as a last resort."

Walter Lippmann, even in 1932 a gray eminence, summed up Mr. Roosevelt as "a pleasant man who, without any important qualifications for the job, would like very much to be president." Once that pleasant man made it to the White House, he put most of his emphasis on sheer experimentation and, well, the Think System. ("The only thing we have to fear is fear itself.") No wonder Ronald Reagan quotes FDR admiringly. Their politics may be generations apart, but they share a vibrant spirit and a talent for communicating it. Both could be described as happy warriors.

Above all, both FDR and The Great Communicator gave the nation a sense of movement, a feeling that the country was coming back strong, even when their critics claimed they were leading the country nowhere but downhill fast. To some, FDR was only That Man, unmentionable by name, a traitor to his class. To some, Ronald Reagan remains a mixture of Ebenezer Scrooge and the missile-slinging cowboy in the *Pravda* cartoons. Yet both to an extent recast the country in their own, smiling image. Not even the *Times* could deny that Mr. Reagan has been proven right about the inextinguishable spirit of America. What a contrast with Jimmy Carter, who seemed obsessed with a capital-M Malaise that proved largely of his own fearful making.

Just what FDR accomplished is as debatable as what Ronald Reagan left behind. But if Franklin Roosevelt didn't save the country, he held it together, mainly with hope and a different program a month, until it could be saved. If Ronald Reagan didn't offer the specific blueprints the *Times* wanted, if he kept stumbling into misstatements, still his spirit was an accurate reflection of the nation's rising hopes. Not even the gloomiest editorials in the *Times* could disguise the comeback of the American dream.

There were other presidential candidates in 1984 doubtless more to the *Times*'s refined tastes—candidates with detailed blueprints and an engineer's control of the technical data. There was such a candidate in 1932, too. He had the plans, the experience, and a host of reforms to his name—the Federal Farm Board and its farm price supports, the Relief and Construction Act, the Reconstruction Finance Corporation, the Federal Home Loan Bank Act . . . and after the campaign was over, he was a broken man. Herbert Hoover declined even to respond to the applause of the crowd as he was driven to his successor's inauguration. He could no longer offer hope, or a new spirit, or the willingness to experiment. Nobody would confuse the eminently practical Mr. Hoover with the Music Man.

In 1984, the *New York Times* was still warning that the Reagan recovery couldn't last, and that the nation's new vigor abroad was only the same old irresponsibility. The good gray *Times* had seldom done more to earn its nickname. In an editorial that could have been written by Chicken Little, it concluded that The End Is Near:

> America is upbeat now, mainly because the business cycle has gone from recession to recovery. Mr. Reagan is skillful at conveying an optimistic mood, but he has not shown how *he's* responsible for it. Worse, his deficit spending can hasten a savage new cycle of inflation and recession. The President offers no program to guard against that and no protection for the victims. Only music.

Only music. But music may be what is most necessary. If it is the music of hope and aspiration, if its seventy-six trombones allow everybody who loves a parade to envision a bright future and start marching toward it, if each marcher can step off in the assurance that the dollars he earns won't turn into funny money and the government he supports won't hold him back—what a parade that could be.

Only music. That's what must be most maddening of all to this president's critics, as it was to FDR's. How dare that man mobilize the whole country around nothing but words and hope, when everybody is supposed to be fearful? There is a group of Americans constitutionally unable to appreciate a Professor Harold Hill. They used to be called Republicans. But before this election year was over, the breed would include many good gray Democrats.

February 10, 1984

38 Brooks Robinson

Reverie on Third

The choice of Brooks Robinson for the Baseball Hall of Fame the first year he was eligible does honor to the judgment of this country's baseball writers. If the political commentators don't know what they're about, at least the baseball writers do. Brooks Robinson, besides being an Arkansas boy and one of the nicest guys around, is about the greatest third baseman who ever lived. It is some comfort in these times of uncertain standards to note the degree of unanimity with which at least one class of public critics can still recognize quality: Brooks Robinson led the baseball writers' poll with 344 of a possible 374 votes.

This vote is also a tribute to third basemen—that peculiar, unglamorous, dignified fraternity. What kid ever started out to be a third baseman? Most young bloods with a yen for the infield have dreams of shortstop, with all the razzmatazz action and constant attention; more mature youngsters with some idea of grace and social dynamics prefer second base. But third? Kids get to be third basemen by some quirk, like having an arm good enough to get the throw to first base every time, even on a bounce, or not having enough sense or speed to get out of the way of a cannonball. Or because nobody else wants to play third.

Then, after a few years at third, or in some cases after only a few innings, something happens. Third base comes into its own. It makes second look like a hole for dabbling esthetes, and shortstop a refuge for hyperactive showoffs. First base remains what it always has been: a place for southpaws and authority figures.

Third is the spot for dormant meditation during epochs of inaction punctuated by moments of truth. All the intense waiting suddenly pays or suddenly kills. And after a time the third baseman begins to treat other players not with contempt—never that—but a bemused tolerance. He looks at them the way a dogface might glance at a beardless kid with a neat forty-mission crease in his brand-new fighter-pilot's cap.

Brooks Robinson played third the way it should be played—without greasepaint or hauteur but with the total absorption that only the beginner mistakes for passivity. The mass of third basemen lead lives of quiet concentration. But underneath the stolidity, beyond the brute numerical logic of a third base and its geometric inevitability in baseball's universe, there is a life of the mind and arm, and moments that surpass grace.

Such a moment came in the sixth inning of the first game of the World Series in 1970. Cincinnati Reds versus the Baltimore Orioles. The Reds are rallying. Lee May up. A wild bouncer down the third-base line. It gets past Robinson. He's after, then over, and somehow on top of it. The ball gets to first on one bounce, thudding safely in Boog Powell's big glove. A double becomes an out. End of rally. Apotheosis of Brooks Robinson, and of third base.

A relief pitcher for the Reds, Clay Carroll, remembers that play of Robinson's (who could forget?): "He was going toward the bullpen when he threw to first. His arm went one way, his body another, and his shoes another." And the ball to first. It was almost incidental that later Brooks Robinson would hit the tie-breaking home run that gave the Orioles the game 4 to 3, and that he would go on to dominate the Series, Baltimore winning in five. That single play has come to symbolize the whole Series and Brooks Robinson. It may not have been poetry, except in the manner of Walt Whitman in chaotic flight, but it was excellence. And perhaps beauty.

Mortimer Adler, the Great Bookie of the Western World, speaks of the three medieval principles of beauty, all of which Brooks Robinson and third basemen in general regularly violate—wholeness, proportion, and clarity. (Well, maybe not clarity. A sudden stop and a throw like a shot can be very clear.) And yet that throw, bounce and all, was beautiful. So there's hope that baseball, though being blitzed at the moment by mindless football, may yet prove a modern sensibility and not a medieval relic.

There is such a thing as beauty of character, too. Brooks Robinson's reaction on being elected to the Hall of Fame his first time up was typical in its consideration: "I am sorry for all the deserving players who didn't make it." That ranks with his response when the Orioles' legendary-in-his-own-time manager, Earl Weaver, finally replaced him at third. "All he said," Earl Weaver recalls "was, 'If you need me, I'll be here.' "

Brooks Robinson was the fielder par excellence, with the highest lifetime fielding average of any third baseman (.971), the most chances, the most assists, the most put-outs, and the most double plays. But it would be wrong, it would be laughable, to dismiss him as Good Field, No Hit. Brooks Robinson's lifetime batting average of .267 looks better and better as modern batting averages dip. But more significant was *when* he hit—in the clutch. If some genius with numbers ever tries to draw up a list of the most dependable batters after the seventh inning with the game on the line, he could use as his statistical model the batting record of Brooks Robinson.

But statistics can't capture the dull-gray mystique of third base. To think of third basemen is to dwell on men slightly apart but there when needed, gentlemen in attendance. They crouch like a rock and spring back like a young pine. They do not believe in being taken by surprise. Brooks Robinson is their exemplar, but there are others who typify the species: Hank Majeski of the old Philadelphia A's and Stanley Hack of the Chicago Cubs. George Kell, another Arkansas boy, who played third for the Detroit Tigers. Eddie Yost and Eddie Matthews. And Pie Traynor. All were watchful and waitful. All were quietly durable. (The loquacious exception, Pepper Martin of the Cards, was a shortstop at heart.) There's no flash to third base. Those who play it must develop the staying power of a boulder, and combine it with eternal vigilance. Third basemen eventually come to share certain traits, like constancy and hitting in the clutches. Perhaps because third base makes the player, and the man, as much as he makes it.

January 16, 1983

39 Tommy Robinson

The Ur-Redneck

Years ago I appeared in a televised debate with another news-paperman and Orval Faubus, a former governor of Arkansas and permanent footnote in American history. (For further details, see Little Rock Crisis of 1957. Or look under Law, Defiance of.) Today I can recall only one thing about that forgettable encounter: At one egregious point, Mr. Faubus compared his calling out troops to oppose the Constitution of the United States with Abraham Lincoln's calling up troops to save it. I believe they could have heard my reaction to that one in Little Rock even if there had been no hookup to my microphone in Pine Bluff. Mercifully, the rest of that discussion is now but a dim blur in my memory. Time heals almost all.

What I do remember distinctly is what happened the day after the program was aired. I got a call bright and early from someone who identified himself as Tommy Robinson. He's now a congress-man, the latest to switch from the Democratic to the Republican party, and is preparing to run for governor of the state. But even then the man was as detested in some quarters as he was popular in others for following his impulses rather than the law.

I was surprised to hear my caller expressing admiration and agreement. I had convinced him, he said, that no man is above the law, and that anyone who takes an oath to uphold it ought to do just that—and that includes following court orders. He sounded like a sudden convert to law and order, the real thing this time.

Not that I thought his mood would last—it didn't—but I've

always remembered that conversation, and conversion. It was so much like Tommy to follow his instincts even on the rare occasion when they were right. Of course he was back court-bashing within days, maybe hours. Conversions can go as suddenly as they come.

A more cynical observer might dismiss that call from Tommy Robinson as sheer hypocrisy. I wouldn't. I have no doubt the man was as sincere at that moment as he would be when he ran for Congress on a platform that consisted largely of cussin' the courts. Some people can raise Cain on Saturday night with as much genuine devotion as they promise to straighten up and fly right Sunday morning—and do it *every* Saturday night and *every* Sunday morning. This is not insincerity. Quite the opposite: it is a vast, enthusiastic surfeit of sincerity that no number of outlets can satisfy.

Folks like Tommy Robinson are the natural enthusiasts of life, and when they become politicians, they turn republics into democracies and democracies into demagogueries. Some demagogues only ape belief; they truly believe only in their own ambition. But the naturals among them tend to believe what they're saying, at least while they're saying it. Tommy Robinson is among the latter. He not only voices his instincts; he acts on them.

Why else would he make a risky run for governor when he had a safe congressional seat? Why not serve another term or two in the House, qualify for a nice pension, and then challenge Arkansas's only challengeable senator, Dale Bumpers, in 1992? That would be the logical course for an ambitious pol to take. But logic is to Tommy Robinson as water is to a duck's back. The reason he is so good at exploiting the instincts of others is that he follows his own.

A more cynical observer might suspect that Tommy Robinson is just playing the game. Why else would he say he became a Republican because he could no longer stomach a party run by the likes of Jesse Jackson when, as a delegate to the Democratic National Convention, he voted to nominate Jesse Jackson for president? Because, of course, to a good ol' boy, any candidate was preferable to Michael Dukakis, a white liberal from Taxachusetts. Besides, a vote for Jesse Jackson would express Tommy's utter contempt for his biggest rival and Dukakis's biggest booster in the state, Governor Bill Clinton. The politics of all that may not be consistent, but the feelings are. The feelings are more than consistent; they're part of one coherent, emotional whole.

Years ago, when I was a graduate student doing a paper on Huey Long, perhaps the greatest demagogue of them all, I visited his elder brother Julius, then an old man in a dingy office in downtown Shreveport. It was a scene out of *All the King's Men*. To the whirl of the slowly oscillating electric fan on the floor, Mr. Julius leaned back, plucked his galluses, and proceeded to explain why his brother had been such a great orator—the second best he'd ever heard, said Julius Long. (The first was Gerald L. K. Smith, for a time Huey's heir apparent before he made a career of anti-Semitism.)

What Huey would do, said Mr. Julius, was go out to the little railroad depots and cotton-weighing platforms of north Louisiana, hit every emotional theme he knew, and wait till the good ol' boys took their hands out of their overalls. When they applauded, Huey knew he had hit the right note. He'd seize on it, add a few variations *agitato* and *crescendo*, and have an oratorical symphony to ride to power.

Nobody will claim that Tommy Robinson has Huey Long's genius. In one respect, he doesn't need it. He doesn't need consultants or polls or rhetorical test runs under a hot sun to find out what the people are thinking. He knows, because he's one of them. He's a natural. He doesn't just *appeal* to the lowest common denominator of the electorate—he's it.

I for one would not want to be represented by someone just like me. I'd prefer someone a lot better. Someone who could overcome my limits, my prejudices, my narrow self-interest—someone who would follow not impulse but judgment. But to voters looking for a politician who will mirror their own unmediated instincts, and act on impulses they might restrain in the light of day, Tommy Robinson's the man. He can say and do things they might not be able to bring themselves to do. He enacts the cherished fantasies of others, and leaves them cheering, at least inwardly.

If the object of representative government were only to be representative, Tommy Robinson would be the perfect candidate in this still essentially populist state. He is the ur-redneck, a personification of both the meanness and, yes, the nobility of that species.

Tommy Robinson is scarcely a model of political stability, with all his sudden swings and strange inconsistencies, but he is a model of emotional integrity.

September 20, 1989

40 Bayard Rustin

A Costly Consistency

All his life, and he was 77 when he died, Bayard Rustin was a protester—and also a powerful force for order. That's what made him the great organizer of the civil-rights movement in this country, which not only revolutionized life in these Southern latitudes but did so peacefully. Has any other culture toppled a formal, deeply rooted caste system with such dispatch and legality? That kind of accomplishment took not only fervor but Bayard Rustin's specialty—organization.

There was an ordinariness and simplicity to the way Bayard Rustin arranged things, and both qualities are reflected in the degree of racial integration in today's South—a degree even the most hopeful and well intentioned might not have foreseen in 1954. Bayard Rustin understood that racial *equality* was not the unnatural imposition on people's lives; racial segregation was. And in a calm, businesslike way, he proceeded to organize its disappearance.

When Martin Luther King, Jr., the Mirabeau of this revolution, decided to bring 200,000 people to Washington in 1963, he naturally turned to Bayard Rustin, his own Lazare Carnot, the French Revolution's "organizer of victory." In a lifetime of organizing protests from Montgomery, Alabama, to New York City, the immense rally at the Lincoln Memorial in August 1963 was Bayard Rustin's greatest challenge—and his greatest victory.

Even many of those who would have liked nothing better than to drive a stake through Jim Crow's cruel old heart had qualms about

142

bringing hundreds of thousands of angry, frustrated Americans to the capital for one great catharsis. The prospect brought back memories of the Bonus March of 1932 and its violence, fires, bayonets. But when this march materialized, it could have been a church service. The image of Abraham Lincoln looked on approvingly as the great congregation prayed, sang, dreamed—and departed. The victory had been organized.

Bayard Rustin put together many another march on behalf of many another cause. He was the one who raised $100,000 for the striking garbage collectors in Memphis when Martin Luther King went there for what would be his last protest, and it was Bayard Rustin who would organize the great and, again, peaceful march to mourn the fallen leader.

Mr. Rustin was called on a few years later to organize a tent city in Washington as part of another protest—the Poor People's Campaign. But he resigned rather than echo slogans about Black Power, which by then had replaced Martin Luther King's dream for all. Bayard Rustin's definition of equality didn't mean that some were more equal than others.

When he deliberately, thoughtfully, broke the law on behalf of a higher one, he deliberately, thoughtfully, went to jail for it. He was a conscientious objector not just by legal status but by vocation. Civil disobedience meant more than a dramatic gesture to Bayard Rustin; it was a discipline, a witness. Wherever he was—on a North Carolina chain gang for participating in the first Freedom Ride ever back in 1947, or in federal prison for resisting the draft during the Second World War—he knew why he was there, and so did others. You didn't have to agree with his principles to know he had them, and was willing to pay for them.

Yes, Bayard Rustin could be suckered. By opposing American policy in Southeast Asia, he became the unwitting accomplice of the genocidal regime that turned Cambodia into one great charnel house. His pacifism would serve the ends of a tyranny that now has plunged all of Vietnam into the kind of unbroken slavery and endless war that appalled Bayard Rustin most of all. But if his convictions misled him on occasion, he always had the courage of them. And he was no party-liner. That became clear when the civil-rights movement ossified into just another pressure group looking after its own. It was no longer the movement he had organized, and he said so.

For an old-time political organizer, it is easy enough to stand up to the old and familiar antagonists, but Bayard Rustin stood up to racism even when it appeared in his own corner. Devoid of ambition in the vulgar sense, he organized crowds; he would not play to them. Nowhere does the record show an instance of his being moved by fear or malice, or even by common opportunism. That kind of consistency can be costly. Having organized the victory, Bayard Rustin, like Lazare Carnot in that other revolution, would be denounced as a reactionary and cast into ideological exile.

The wire services, trying to pigeonhole his political affiliation, identified Bayard Rustin as a moderate rather than a radical. They were mistaken. There is nothing more radical than someone who will follow his principles where they lead. Bayard Rustin was radical enough to insist on fairness not only for his own but for others; how many of today's "radicals" would go that far? It is expected in a political organizer that he will not be bullied by his opponents, but Bayard Rustin would not be bullied even by friends in whose cause he had fought.

When asked what he believed in, Mr. Rustin had a litany he would recite: non-violence, democratic procedures, respect for human personality, and the oneness of man. In a lifetime of actions that were more eloquent than words, he witnessed for all those beliefs—through freedom and captivity, in youth and age. On his death, he bequeathed not just a great victory organized but an elemental decency. That is no small thing after a career devoted to fighting intensely for principle. As George Orwell once wrote of another believer in non-violence, Mohandas K. Gandhi (for whose ideas, incidentally, he had no great enthusiasm): " . . . regarded simply as a politician, and compared with the other leading figures of our time, how clean a smell he has managed to leave behind!"

August 29, 1987

41 Raoul Salan

For His Crimes and His Services

After a lifetime of heroism and something less, General Raoul Salan died quietly of old age at the Val de Grace Hospital in Paris at 85. The French never could decide whether to give him the *Croix de Guerre* or a court-martial, and in the end wound up giving him both, in roughly that order.

Raoul Albin Louis Salan from near Toulouse, graduate of St. Cyr, earned the *Croix de Guerre*, the first of his thirty-six military decorations, fighting for the Third Republic during the First World War. At the onset of the Second, he sided with Vichy—an early indication of regrettable tendencies that would later surface, not to say explode. He switched to the Free French when the tide changed, fighting with distinction in the invasion of southern France.

During the Fourth Republic, he took command of French forces in Algeria, where he carried out his orders to keep the peace in so correct and impartial a manner that he was suspected of being insufficiently sympathetic to the French settlers and became the target of a right-wing assassination plot. That was before right-wing assassination plots became his own specialty.

The Fifth Republic (the French have to number theirs) was the one General Salan helped create by rallying, like most other Frenchmen, to the call of Charles de Gaulle. But when the Knight of Lorraine turned out to favor an orderly departure of the French from Algeria, General Salan retired and took up a new hobby: defiance. Exiled to Spain in 1960, he set up a society for retired generals—the Secret Army Organization, a group dedicated to

145

keeping Algeria French, or at least in smithereens. The general developed a new interest: *plastiques*. That's how Algeria became a forerunner of Beirut in senseless destruction, and the SAO a precursor of the PLO's kind of chivalry.

For four days in April 1961, Raoul Salan and three fellow generals actually seized control of Algiers in a kind of Gallic Tet. But the SAO was quickly subdued—not so much by French arms as by French words. In language that can still set even an American to humming the "Marseillaise," General de Gaulle broadcast an appeal to Algeria. The historic voice on the radio implored Frenchmen not to fire on their compatriots but to rally once again to the mother country. After that, only mopping-up operations were required.

Raoul Salan fled before the onrush of words and arms. He was found guilty of treason and sentenced to death in absentia, which is how the sentence was carried out, too, since after his capture his punishment was successively lightened. He was given life imprisonment for his part in a plot to assassinate General de Gaulle, that is, the Fifth Republic. Six years later, he would be pardoned by De Gaulle himself. Later another president of the republic, François Mitterand, would restore General Salan's rank and pension.

Undecided whether to punish Raoul Salan for his crimes or reward him for his services, the Fifth Republic proved itself French by doing both. His treatment was a triumph of Gallic reason, exhibiting both prudence and charity, which in such circumstances can be identical. It was Raoul Salan's destiny to serve as a reminder of the statesmanship and magnanimity of others. From this distance, long removed from the fire and blood, there is something almost comical in misadventures that were once so serious.

Americans have had our Raoul Salans, too. One was named Edwin A. Walker. Remember him? He served his country long and well, if not long or well enough. In 1957, he led the 101st Airborne in exemplary fashion when Dwight Eisenhower dispatched it to carry out the law of the land in Little Rock. The constitutional challenge that Orval Faubus initiated that year was met with dispatch and professionalism. General Walker and his troopers tolerated no nonsense.

Only five years later, Edwin A. Walker would take up a sad and curious stance on the other side of the Constitution he had sworn to uphold; he was the most prominent protester on campus when Ole Miss was integrated by court order. The general had joined the side of defiance. He wound up barnstorming the country in the Billy James Hargis show, a right-wing touring company in the sixties. Last time I saw him, he was on exhibit in Little Rock's Robinson Auditorium, co-starring with Billy James.

How account for Edwin Walker's strange trajectory, his dual career as professional soldier and wooden demagogue? Was it tragedy or farce? His destiny, too, was to challenge the wisdom and demonstrate the forbearance of others. Jerry Neill, a great editorial writer for the old *Arkansas Gazette*, summed it up for the ages when he casually identified Edwin A. Walker as "the Raoul Salan of the Texas League." It was a definitive judgment on two lives.

July 20, 1984

42 Sydney Schanberg

A Verb Is Born

Schanberg (shan-burg), *v.i.* [American Eng.; from American journalist Sydney S., who failed to foresee holocaust in Cambodia, circa 1975.] 1. To fail to sense evil, its presence and potential. 2. To make excuses for such failure. 3. Both of the above.

For the record it should be noted that Sydney H. Schanberg has admitted he was wrong about Cambodia. Who is Sydney H. Schanberg? He's the correspondent for the *New York Times* who was so sadly, monstrously, repeatedly wrong about what would happen in Cambodia after a Communist victory there that he got a Pulitzer Prize for it. He was prophesying a better, even glowing future for the Cambodians even as the holocaust there got under way. Ever since, his copy has been cited with delectation by aficionados of hubris as the prize-winning example of gliberal blindness about Communist intentions—and capabilities.

Now Sydney Schanberg himself, in a letter to a conservative quarterly, the Heritage Foundation's *Policy Review*, owns up to having been wrong about Cambodia, kind of: "Virtually all Cambodians living in government-held areas and most members of the press corps believed, despite the wartime brutality of the Khmer Rouge, that these Cambodian Communists would—once they had achieved victory—see no further purpose in random killing and would opt instead for reconciliation with their fellow Cambodians. . . . The instant this belief proved to be wrong, I and others said we had been wrong, loudly and clearly. and I have been saying it loudly and clearly ever since—in articles and statements."

This is the first time, despite all those loud and clear articles and statements, that Mr. Schanberg's apology has come to my attention, but that is scarcely his fault. After Cambodia, the sight of his byline did not move me to continue reading.

Gentle Reader will note that Sydney Schanberg's apology is more of an apologia, with its assertion that "virtually all Cambodians living in government-held areas and most members of the press corps" made the same terrible mistake he did. They, of course, might not have had his direct access to the *New York Times* and therefore his power to spread his misimpressions worldwide. As in his (in)famous report four days before the fall of Phnom Penh that, for "ordinary people of Indochina . . . it is difficult to imagine how their lives could be anything but better with the Americans gone." That failure of imagination was soon more than compensated for by unspeakable reality.

Even when the executions got under way, Sidney Schanberg was assuring his readers that "none of this will apparently bear any resemblance to the mass executions that had been expected by many Westerners." It is still uncertain just how many millions were killed in Cambodia, but it's estimated that a third of the country's population was done to death. A third.

David Roberts, Jr., of Social Democrats USA compiled a sampler of such Schanbergisms for *Policy Review*. That's what inspired Mr. Schanberg's response, including this not very graceful apology, which was tucked away within a longer and even more self-serving letter to the editor. Perhaps the tendency to rationalize one's worst mistakes reflects not politics so much as a gap in social training. It is rare now, and not just in political circles, to find people who can apologize simply, without sharing the blame, or trying to excuse themselves, or saying "I'm sorry, but . . ." with the emphasis on the *but*. Mr. Schanberg's problem may really be one not for a political critic but for Miss Manners.

Sydney Schanberg writes that he was wrong *but* most other members of the press corps made the same mistake. If only he had subscribed to a column written from a key listening post like Pine Bluff, Arkansas, he might not have been surprised at the impending bloodbath in Southeast Asia. It may seem surprising that a danger so vast should be invisible to those so close to it, and so clear to someone at a distance. But travel can be narrowing, too.

Distance lends perspective. The distant observer is obliged to depend not only on his own limited impressions but on the experience of others and even of other generations—in short, on a sense of history. Sydney Schanberg might have been able to see the ominous shadow cast by events to come in Cambodia if he had been dispatched not to Phnom Penh but to the New York Public Library to read Hannah Arendt on *The Origins of Totalitarianism*, or Robert Conquest's classic history of Stalin's purges and collectivizations (its title would apply as well to events in Cambodia): *The Great Terror*.

Sydney Schanberg was *not* wrong about one thing: many shared his misperceptions. The next issue of *Policy Review* contained a select list of those false prophecies, including these gems:

· "Some will find the whole bloodbath debate unreal. What future possibility could be more terrible than the reality of what is happening to Cambodia now?"—Anthony Lewis in the *New York Times* on St. Patrick's Day, 1975. His rhetorical question would be answered soon enough, and in the grimmest way.

"The greatest gift our country can give to the Cambodian people is not guns but peace. And the best way to accomplish that goal is by ending military aid now."—Representative (now Senator) Christopher Dodd of Connecticut on March 12, 1975.

"The evidence is that in Cambodia the much-heralded bloodbath that was supposed to follow the fall of Phnom Penh has not taken place."—*The Nation*, June 14, 1975, even while the bloodbath was taking place.

"Indochina Without Americans/For Most, A Better Life"—*New York Times*, April 13, 1975.

Why record such blithe effusions? Do they represent anything now except an exercise in gallows humor? Yes, they represent a warning. Because many of these same sources now give equally eloquent advice about American policy in another decade, and about other small countries, Nicaragua being perhaps the most prominent example. There, too, various beneficences may be expected if Communist rule goes unchallenged. When this same old counsel is offered by these same old counselors, it ought to carry a warning label: Remember the source. And the record.

August 21, 1985

43 Albert Speer

... *But He Was a Great Manager*

Albert Speer was the most educated and civilized, the most articulate and interesting, and in his judgments and writings, perhaps the fairest of the Nazi war criminals tried at Nuremberg. If one could understand Albert Speer, one might be able to understand the tragedy of modern Germany. Most nations have produced their demagogues and demons, their Hitlers and Himmlers, but how explain why, in the Germany of this century, the "decent" people, the supposedly educated and civilized, not only followed their demons but aided and abetted them? Yes, to understand Albert Speer would be to understand modern Germany.

But how understand Herr Speer? Here was an administrative genius, a wizard at production who seemed indifferent much of the time to how the products would be used. He was, in the phrase of British historian H. R. Trevor-Roper, a "moral neuter." He went from being Adolf Hitler's personal architect to minister of armaments and then manager of the whole German war economy— without betraying any sign of the fanatic. He stood out in Hitler's coterie like a calm executive in a menagerie of zealots.

In the midst of the war, the *London Observer* produced a profile of Albert Speer that may still be the best description of his type, and why it is so important to understand it:

Speer is, in a sense, more important for Germany today than Hitler, Himmler, Göring, Goebbels, or the generals. They all have, in a way, become the mere auxiliaries of the man who actually directs the giant power machine—charged with drawing from it the maximum effort under maximum strain. . . . In him is the very epitome of the "managerial revolution."

Speer is not one of the flamboyant and picturesque Nazis. Whether he has any other than conventional political opinions at all is unknown. He might have joined any other political party which gave him a job and a career. He is very much the successful average man, well dressed, civil, non-corrupt, very middle-class in his style of life, with a wife and six children. Much less than any of the other German leaders does he stand for anything particularly German or particularly Nazi. He rather symbolizes a type which is becoming increasingly important in all belligerent countries: the pure technician, the classless bright young man without background, with no other original aim than to make his way in the world and no other means than his technical and managerial ability. It is the lack of psychological and spiritual ballast, and the ease with which he handles the terrifying technical and organizational machinery of our age, which makes this slight type go extremely far nowadays. . . . This is their age; the Hitlers and Himmlers we may get rid of, but the Speers, whatever happens to this particular special man, will long be with us.

Albert Speer made a point of jokingly showing Hitler a translation of this article in the *Observer* before any of his rivals in that mad court could present it as evidence of his un-Nazi demeanor. Der Führer read it all the way through, then handed it back, according to Albert Speer, with great respect. It was the tribute of one generation of the Nazi revolution to the next, the tribute of ideologue to technocrat. Hitler might as well have handed over a fistful of ashes, for that is all that would remain of the New Germany he and his architect were going to construct together.

Albert Speer should have suspected as much from Der Führer's taste in architecture; his boss always wanted young Speer to design buildings that would make magnificent ruins. That was the essence of Hitler's idea of architecture. The ruins came soon enough: the thousand-year Reich lasted little more than a decade.

How did Albert Speer get suckered, or sucker himself? Why did he join the Nazi party almost frivolously, on a whim, without studying party programs or political questions? He would never have approved an ordinary blueprint so casually. Later, he would be given twenty years to think on the question. And in his memoirs, he would conclude:

> As an intellectual I might have been expected to collect documentation with the same thoroughness and to examine various points of view with the same lack of bias that I had learned to apply to my preliminary architectural studies. This failure was rooted in my inadequate political schooling. As a result, I remained uncritical, unable to deal with the arguments of my student friends, who were predominantly indoctrinated with the National Socialist ideology.
>
> For had I only wanted to, I could have found out even then that Hitler was proclaiming expansion of the Reich to the east; that he was a rank anti-Semite; that he was committed to a system of authoritarian rule; that after attaining power he intended to eliminate democratic procedures and would thereafter yield only to force. Not to have worked that out for myself; not, given my education, to have read books, magazines, and newspapers of various viewpoints; not to have tried to see through the whole apparatus of mystification—was already criminal.

The next time you hear it said that not everyone need study politics, particularly to become only a technician, or an executive, or a mere voter, think on Albert Speer. Think on Germany.

Herr Speer's memoirs, like his other products, are detailed, efficient, and craftsmanlike. But after all the layers of description and explanation are peeled off, there is only a void, an emotional emptiness, at the core. As late as 1944, when he was doubtless the biggest employer of slave labor on the European continent, and when hundreds of thousand of human beings were being worked to death at his direction, Herr Speer could write this memorandum to his Führer: "The task I have to fulfill is an unpolitical one. I have felt at ease in my work only so long as my person and my work were evaluated solely by the standard of practical accomplishments."

The full grotesquerie of his attitude would not strike him until after the war; he had allowed the work ethic to drive out all other ethics. As he would write later: "I did not see any moral ground outside the system where I should have taken my stand." His was a terrifying kind of innocence.

Despite the formal confessions, and a post-facto high-mindedness exceptional in the literature of Naziism, Albert Speer's memoirs remain unmoving. His writing is as effective, and as soul-less, as his administration was. And as successful: his books were best sellers. Albert Speer was able to make even confession a successful enterprise.

After all his words, Albert Speer remains at least as mysterious, and as inhuman in his own way, as Adolf Hitler. And the thought occurs that the Speers may be far more numerous than the Hitlers, and far more dangerous in an age of technology. It is an age in which vast projects may be launched and miraculous inventions employed without much attention to the question: To what end?

September 12, 1981

44 I. F. Stone

From Gadfly to Institution

It is still hard to see the name I. F. Stone, even in an obituary, without mentally adding *'s Weekly*. For almost twenty years, from 1953 to 1972, *I. F. Stone's Weekly* was what a political newsletter should be: densely written, highly personal, completely independent, sporadically witty, sometimes almost poetic, and altogether the reflection of the universe that was one writer's idiosyncratic world view. If that perspective didn't always reflect reality, it always reflected I. F. Stone, and he was the reason one bought it—not to see the world but to see it through the eyes of this beady-eyed little New Yorker with the thick glasses, insatiable curiosity, and utter integrity.

"I think he was one of the best commentators on the Washington scene we ever had," said J. William Fulbright, the Distinguished Former from Arkansas. Well, I. F. Stone sure had J. William's high-tone number. Those of us back in Arkansas who had the half-duty, half-obsession to cover Mr. Fulbright will always be envious of the book-review-*cum*-masterpiece that Izzy Stone published on December 29, 1966: "An American Anthony Eden." Of all the phrases used to sum up J. William Fulbright's distance from things essentially American, I. F. Stone had come up with just the right one. And of course he had gone to England, the spiritual home of Fulbrightism, for the perfect analogue: Anthony Eden, too, had known early glory and matured into stylish irrelevance.

Technically, the essay was a review of Tris Coffin's worshipful biography of the senator, but I. F. Stone saw through the book

156

from the outset. It was, he said, a "panegyric almost to the point of caricature . . . advertising copy, not serious writing." Then he proceeded to review not the book but J. William Fulbright with devastating insight. Izzy Stone understood that when Fulbright stood up on historic occasion to a Joe McCarthy or J. Edgar Hoover, it was out of gentlemanly disdain and nothing so vulgar or American or uncontrollable as moral principle. ("Though Fulbright once taught constitutional law, it never seems to have permeated his marrow.") Hence the senator's support for the Southern Manifesto and associated rot. His gentleman's code was the source of both his finest minutes and his most disappointing hours. Izzy Stone realized as much, early, and said it, clearly.

Seldom has the Fulbrightesque *modus operandi*, with its condescension toward the public and chumminess with power, been better described than in I. F. Stone's book review and cultural evisceration. Another example: "Tris Coffin's hero-worshiping portrait achieves its highest level of unrecognizability in calling Fulbright a modern Prometheus. Fulbright would never have done anything so irregular as stealing fire for Man. He would have sent Zeus a carefully prepared but private memorandum suggesting that it would be better to give man fire than risk the tumultuous uprising sure to be provoked by cold meats on a rumbling stomach." That's I. F. Stone. And that's J. William Fulbright.

That Fulbright, with his tendency to speak polite nothings to power, should have emerged at one semi-chaotic time (the sixties) as a hero of the New Left was as amusing as that Izzy Stone should have. If Fulbright wasn't Old Right, he was at least Old Rentier, as I. F. Stone detected in his essay. And I. F. Stone would never have passed for a Flower Child. His politics were classic Old Left, and his work habits would have made the average middle-class burgher look like a layabout. If Izzy Stone had had a motto emblazoned on his escutcheon, it would have been: Never Trust the Bastards. As the *Washington Post* noted when he finally put aside his battered typewriter, I. F. Stone may have been "the only Marxist ever to make good as a capitalist in the fiercely competitive jungle of American free-enterprise journalism."

I. F. Stone got his scoops the old-fashioned way—by dutifully reading every word of the small type in completely public reports.

He parsed close-set congressional debates, committee minutes, and other stultifying stuff that any mod journalist would chuck en route to his rendezvous with Deep Throat. I. F. Stone was no journalist; he was a newspaperman—a digger, an explainer, to whom passion wasn't a mood but life.

When he finally retired to study Greek and get the inside scoop on Socrates, it was so he could expose that cultural artifact as an enemy of the state and a snob who was always asking cynical questions (which is pretty much what an Athenian court found) and whose marriage wasn't so hot, either. I. F. Stone may have stopped publishing his *Weekly*, but he stayed in the muckraking line. You didn't have to agree with Mr. Stone (thank goodness) to be perpetually delighted with him, as he was with life.

Now and then he even rose to bad poetry, as in his description of what the Vietnam War was really about in "More than Steel and Chrome Could Bear," written in February 1967:

> It is the Machine, it is the prestige of the Machine that is at stake in Vietnam. It is Boeing and General Electric and Goodyear and General Dynamics. It is the electronic rangefinder and the amphibious truck and the night-piercing radar. It is the defoliant, and the herbicide, and the deodorant, and the depilatory. It is the products and the brand names we have been conditioned since childhood to revere. . . . Down there in the jungles, unregenerate, ingenious, tricky, as tiny as a louse or a termite, and as hard to get out, emerged a strange creature whose potency we had almost forgotten—Man. To sit down and deal with him is to admit that the Machine has lost to Man, that our beautifully computerized war, with the most complicated devices for killing ever assembled and the most overwhelming firepower ever mustered, has failed.

To read I. F. Stone's journalism was a little like reading Ezra Pound's poetry; it was interesting, almost moving, but something was lacking—a certain ring of truth?—because something was always in the way—ideology? Only later would it become clearer, after the re-education camps and the killing fields and the Boat People, which forces represented Man in Southeast Asia and which the dull, brutal machine that kills not just body but mind and soul. Only later still may it become clear that Vietnam was lost not in

Vietnam but somewhere else—on television screens, in newspaper columns, in the circuitous clauses of the Pentagon's Rules of (non)Engagement, and in the irresolution of politicians that betrayed the resolution of soldiers. The war was lost in the hearts and minds not of Vietnamese but of Americans.

There can be no doubt that I. F. Stone was always true to his own vision, however narrow. "To thine own self be true, and it must follow, as the night the day, thou canst not then be false to any man" may have been the most dangerous of Polonius's misunderstandings.

On those days when his eye was sharp, unclouded by his favorite fixations, I. F. Stone had no betters. He saw his own future sharply when, decades back, he told his wife, Esther, circulation manager and production assistant of the *Weekly*, that "if I lived long enough I'd graduate from a pariah to a character, and then if I lasted long enough, from character to public institution." He did. It was a long and happy rise, or maybe decline, from the days when *I. F. Stone's Weekly* at $5 an annual throw was a kind of private club. At the end, he had attained his more recent and elevated status as cultural icon. It was the difference between the old Garrison Keillor of Minnesota and the new one from New York. Once official folk-hero status is conferred, something is gone—as I. F. Stone well knew, and could even see coming. He was prescient about politics if not ideas.

On his death, it is still the *Weekly* that one misses most, and the direct hits he would score often enough to keep even opposite-but-equally-dogmatic types reading, or at least skimming. The First Amendment will never be completely satisfactory until every shade of opinion has its own I. F. Stone.

June 30, 1989

45 Jimmy Swaggart

The Show Goes On

In all the hubbub about Jimmy Swaggart, professional evangelist and repentant, where is the concern for the prostitute he is supposed to have sinned with? Where are the tearful embraces, outreaching arms, painful sighs, heartfelt forgiveness, glorious reconciliation, and full television coverage for her? No one seems to be concerned about *her* feelings, *her* pain. The spotlight is always on Brother Swaggart, who seems to have fallen from the heights of publicity to the heights of publicity, while the prostitute remains only The Prostitute, a stock figure, not a person to be confronted, loved, forgiven, embraced. She is being sought only by those two relentless avengers of our society, the police and the press.

In his time, the Teacher from Nazareth was notoriously easy on prostitutes by the standards of his day, which have not changed all that much in ours. For that matter, the Bible speaks of prostitutes in many other contexts; often they play the role of heroine. But they are treated as persons, not foils.

Tamar, who plays the whore to her father-in-law Judah, is clearly justified in the thirty-eighth chapter of Genesis, one of the most beautiful, sensuous, rich, dramatic, and condensed tales in The Book—a single, shimmering story dropped unaccountably into the saga of Joseph, like white gold on yellow. In Hosea, the prostitute Gomer becomes the symbol of the wayward but divinely loved.

But what has this or any other religious theme to do with the Jimmy Swaggart Show? His saga is a lot closer to *True Confessions* than Holy Scripture. Jimmy Swaggart is still The Star; the prosti-

160

tute is but the means of Our Hero's downfall rather than a subject of concern herself. Yet she prostitutes only her body; what is one to make of someone who prostitutes the spirit?

Long before this episode, Jimmy Swaggart had come to symbolize the latest substitute for the spiritual in these high-tech times: televangelism.

Once upon a time, a kind of ultimate Southern experience was to drive a '54 Chevy down a bayou-fringed highway in the early morning hours, listening to Garner Ted on the radio while the sultry air whooshed past and the bugs splattered on the windshield. At least it was *we* who sweated then; we did sacrifice something. Now we recline in air-conditioned comfort to watch Jimmy Swaggart pace back and forth and offer up all the outward signs of conviction—tears, sweat, and a remarkably precise Spanish translation. Talk about vicarious salvation: his signs of discomfort were our assurance. Anybody who sweated like that had to be sincere.

Marvin Gorman, who ABC says provided the photographs that were shown to the church fathers, is a rival televangelist who shares what is now the most American of relationships with Jimmy Swaggart: acrimonious litigation. Now Brother Gorman can smile the smile of a Christian with an ace up his sleeve. Whether visiting a prostitute is a step above or below distributing pictures of someone who does is one of those points of judgment that the church's discipline may not cover.

Let it be noted that Jimmy Swaggart is in trouble because he visited a prostitute, not because of his bigotry-laced theology, or the way he can mix an intense concern for the letter of the law with a burlesque of its spirit, or the mean, narrow use to which he has put a remarkable gift—his complete mastery of that great spoken tongue, Southern Vulgar. His church would seem to be concerned only with the least of Jimmy Swaggart's sins.

Long before now, Brother Swaggart had a way of turning every subject he touched into soap opera; now he specializes in titillation instead of inspiration. He remains as entertaining, and as boring, as ever. Those who were fascinated with his sermons are probably just as fascinated with his scandals. And he'll pick up a vast new audience of those who thrive on cynicism and spiritual voyeurism. The church elders in Louisiana recommended that Brother Swaggart be barred from preaching for three months, although the usual disciplinary process calls for a year's leave from the pulpit. But how many other ministers in the denomination head a ministry that brings in an estimated $142 million a year?

There's a big demand out there for televangelists. Watching them is so much easier than actually attending church, where you have to deal with three-dimensional people with all their crotchets and demands and everydayness. That can be a drag, like feeding the hungry and clothing the naked. Religion off the screen may have its moments on the mountaintop, but most of the time it's down in that same old valley, and not always with Nice People.

Jimmy Swaggart never leaves the mountain, even when he's down. Of course, his mountain is more of a mountain resort where something entertaining and sentimental and capital-I Inspiring is always happening—a kind of Grossinger's-on-the-tube, *mutatis mutandis*. It's a private little refuge in our own living room or Naugahyded den, where prayer need not involve mundane sacrifice, repentance is freed from atonement, ritual doesn't get in the way, and nothing is ever dull. It's the condensed, *Reader's Digest* version of convenient, trouble-free American religion. You don't have to worry about being bothered by other human beings. No salesman will call.

A news item from the *Arizona Republic* may be apropos. The headline reads: "Daily prayer gets heave-ho as trial in Senate nears." The story, by Deborah Shanahan, begins: "State senators received a memorandum last week informing them that the daily prayer was being discontinued for the duration of Governor Evan Mecham's impeachment trial." After all, this is real, this is earnest, this is an impeachment, a Legal Proceeding. This is no place for empty ritual.

Some of us may share the immediate reaction of a state senator from Phoenix, one Wayne Stump: "This seems like a strange time to start winging it." But for those who understand that religion has its place—on television, along with all the other specials—dispensing with the opening prayer makes sense. This is real life. Jimmy Swaggart, on the other hand, is going to be the subject of much entertaining coverage, innumerable jokes, and staunch defenses from the True Believers. That's show biz. It'll be religion when someone cares about the prostitute.

March 3, 1988

46 Raoul Wallenberg

Waiting for Wallenberg

I was standing in line at the Moscow Airport in 1983, and I was nervous. All I wanted was to leave. In the map pocket of my blue parka, the zipper hidden by a flap, were all my notes gathered during weeks of traveling and talking. There was nothing wrong or revealing on the sheets of yellow, legal-size paper. No names or addresses of dissenters; all had been committed to memory. But I knew there didn't have to be anything wrong for Soviet customs to seize documents. When I entered the country, everything I had with me was handled, inspected, probed.

The line was moving swiftly, and soon I would be out. Then it stopped. In front of me was another member of our group, a newspaper publisher from Red Wing, Minnesota. Phil Duff was explaining that, when we arrived at Leningrad last month, customs had seized some of his books. He had been told that such literature was not allowed in the Soviet Union but that it would be returned when he left the country from Moscow. Now he wanted his books. I groaned inwardly. All I wanted was to get me and my notes on the next Aeroflot out. Forget about the books, man. Where did Phil think he was, Minneapolis?

The customs official, a woman, looked puzzled. Phil explained again. Trying to pacify the American, she said the books would be mailed to him. No, he insisted, he had been told they would be returned when he left. She called over an official from the next counter. No, he couldn't help. Phil produced his receipt. The two studied it. Ah yes, they agreed, they would keep the receipt and be sure to send him the books. In that case, said Phil, just make a photocopy for him. I had to smile at that—as if the Russians, who license even typewriters, kept photocopiers around for the convenience of visiting Americans.

I was beginning to feel my collection of notes form a thick, very visible bulge under my arm that said: Seize Me. One of the customs officers disappeared. Come on, I told Phil, forget it. No, he wanted his books. He would not move.

The other line was proceeding along. We waited. And waited. Then the official came back, and he was carrying—Phil's books. Wrapped in a neat package, with his name on them. Almost every day I spent in the Soviet Union brought some kind of surprise, but none more surprising than that. Phil took the books, nodded goodbye, smiled, and moved on. Just like Minneapolis.

The wait for Raoul Wallenberg's personal effects to emerge out of the Soviet bureaucracy has taken a little longer. Forty-five years after the Swedish attaché disappeared as the Red Army entered Budapest, the KGB has produced the documents he was carrying when taken into custody—his driver's license, an address book in his handwriting, and the blue diplomatic passport stamped with the three crowns of Sweden. Inside the passport was a photograph of the balding 32-year-old architect who would emerge as one of the authentic heroes of the Holocaust.

In 1944, Raoul Wallenberg had volunteered to leave safe, secure Stockholm and attach himself to the Swedish legation in Budapest. As soon as he arrived, he began renting buildings, declaring them Swedish territory, and filling them with hunted Jews. He put together a staff of 300 volunteers to feed, clothe, and hide the fugitives. He gave them special Swedish passports as fast as he could sign his name. "This is Swedish territory," he told an armed patrol that tried to seize his charges. "If you want to take them you will have to shoot me first." When his passports were declared invalid by the Hungarian government, he warned of fictive diplomatic repercussions, and the government relented. He pulled his "Swedish citizens" off deportation trains and out of death marches. By bluff and pretext and threat, he managed to save the 20,000 Jews in his custody.

The example of Raoul Wallenberg made it possible for others—

the Swiss, Spanish, and Portuguese legations and the papal nun-cio—to protect another 20,000. Wallenberg stood off Nazi troops and their Hungarian allies. In a personal confrontation with the SS commander in Budapest, he pointedly mentioned the possibility of war-crimes trials after the fighting was over; a plan to destroy the Jewish ghetto in Budapest and its 70,000 people was never carried out. Tens of thousands of Jews perished, but when the Red Army finally entered the city, some 120,000 had survived. Toward the end, the Nazis and the fanatics of Hungary's Arrow Cross party saw through his bluff and began searching for the Swedish diplo-mat; he evaded arrest by moving to a different house each night.

Raoul Wallenberg must have breathed a sigh of relief when the Russians arrived, not knowing that they would accomplish what the Fascists couldn't. He was last seen January 17, 1945, leaving for Red Army headquarters at Debrecen to get help. The Soviets claimed no knowledge of his whereabouts until 1957, when they announced he had died of a heart attack in Moscow's dreaded Lubyanka prison ten years before.

But other prisoners have reported seeing Raoul Wallenberg alive and in reasonably good condition as late as 1975. He would be 77 now. Nina Lagergren of the Raoul Wallenberg Association in Stockholm believes he is still somewhere in the Soviet gulag, being held in isolation.

It took forty-five years for the KGB to find Raoul Wallenberg's papers. Now let them find him. Some of us are prepared to wait. He did not abandon others; we are not going to abandon him, or his memory. Phil Duff had the right idea.

October 25, 1989

47 Robert Penn Warren

Death of a Native Son

Long ago, in Kentucky, I, a boy, stood
By a dirt road in first dark and heard
The great geese hoot northward.
I could not see them, there being no moon
And the stars sparse. I heard them.
I did not know what was happening in my
*   heart.*
It was the season before the elderberry blooms,
Therefore they were going north.
The sound was passing northward.

                                    —R.P.W.

The day before Robert Penn Warren died, a couple of editorial
writers were playing catch-up at their national convention,
held this year in St. Paul, Minnesota. "What are you reading these
days?" asked one. "Nothing new," said the other, a woman from
Connecticut. "But I'm reading a wonderful old book. *All the King's
Men*. I was telling a friend about it, and all she said was, 'Oh, I read
that in high school.' "

Robert Penn Warren wrote many books but one great book. As
happens with great works, it is reborn on another level when reread
in later life. To read *All the King's Men* in high school or college, or
to see the movie with Broderick Crawford and Mercedes Mc-
Cambridge, is one experience; to reread the book forty years later,

not only at a different age but *in* a different age, is a quite different experience.

The book endures, and grows in the reader's consciousness, largely because its characters are not just types. Willie Stark, Jack Burden, and Sadie Burke are people, and so are Sugar Boy and poor Anne and Adam Stanton, and Judge Irwin and Mortimer L. Littlepaugh. Perhaps they are real because this work of art was based on another work of art, and of nature: Huey Pierce Long. Not that Willie Stark was Huey—Willie was and remains Willie, and is reflected even now in some politicians who come through a Southern editor's door every election year. It is not necessary to have read *All the King's Men* to sound as though one just stepped out of it.

Long after Robert Penn Warren had graduated from truth to fame, from writer to poet laureate, from LSU to Yale, it was reported that a history professor digging into the archives in search of the true Kurt Waldheim, if there is such a creature, had come across documents that tied an obscure lieutenant in the Wehrmacht to certain atrocities in the Balkans. And the best description of the indescribable mixture of exhilaration and pity the professor must have felt on that occasion is to be found in *All the King's Men*. They are the words of Jack Burden—words true and false, dramatic and mundane, sincere and sardonic—after our hero makes his discovery about the old judge:

> So I had it after all the months. For nothing is lost, nothing is ever lost. There is always the clue, the canceled check, the smear of lipstick, the footprint in the canna bed, the condom on the park path, the twitch in the old wound, the baby shoes dipped in bronze, the taint in the blood stream. And all times are one time, and all those dead in the past never lived before our definition gives them life, and out of the shadow their eyes implore us. That is what all of us historical researchers believe. And we love the truth.

The exact words catch the inexact feeling, a mixture of discrete parts yet one perfectly conforming whole. Robert Penn Warren achieved connotation by denotation. Note this jewel of a poem called "After the Dinner Party"—

The last log is black. White ash beneath displays
No last glow. You snuff candles. Soon the old stairs
Will creak with your grave and synchronized tread as each
*   mounts*
To a briefness of light, then true weight of darkness, and then
That heart-dimness in which neither joy nor sorrow counts.
Even so, one hand gropes out for another again.

Robert Penn Warren did much before and after *All the King's Men*. He helped start the *Southern Review*, which fought the good fight against the literary deconstructionists of its time. He and his fellow Fugitives, as his band of literary rebels was styled, reasserted the central place of the work itself in the study of literature—rather than the writer's class, or politics, or suicidal impulses. (Would that someone could do the same for American literature now.) He wrote a silly, condescending chapter on race for that classic manifesto of Southern agrarianism, *I'll Take My Stand*, and matured sufficiently to be embarrassed by it. He was lionized, but not spoiled. He remained a great, if sometimes too obvious, rhetorician.

Now is not the time to dwell on what else Robert Penn Warren might have given the South and the country if he had not chosen to depart, first to snowy Minnesota and then to New England's rocky soil. His second wife suggested they settle in the South. "But I discovered it wasn't the same world," he explained. That is what others who have left say, not dallying over the possibility that their leaving changed it, and themselves. And so the sound of his words passed northward.

He did leave us a great book, and that is almost enough.

September 25, 1989

48 George Washington

The Sound of Distant Music

George Washington remains the most admired and remote of American presidents, more portrait than person. He intended it that way. Like the other founding fathers, he was set on independence—for himself and for his countrymen. To him, independence did not mean indulgence. It meant dignity, decorum, and, yes, distance. It meant a republic whose ungilded honor would tower above the transient monarchies of Europe. America's republican simplicity would exemplify a new order of the ages.

Washington did not propose to fulfill so audacious an agenda by appearing audacious. He would be neither courtier nor demagogue. Rather, he proposed to conduct himself as a citizen of a republic, the first citizen of the first republic to endure. No small ambition, for himself or his country.

No one ever described George Washington as folksy. He dared not forget what he represented. He represented America, and the American idea—that liberty and authority, freedom and order, could dwell together. At the end of the eighteenth century, that notion was sufficient to inspire snickers from tories of every nationality: even if this colonial rabble managed to win a brief independence, imagine it trying to govern itself.

There was reason, even necessity, for Washington's reserve, for his insistence on the formalities and courtesies, on the powdered wig and dress sword, on the proper ceremonies and correct form of address. He had his and the republic's dignity to think of, and at the time they were much the same thing.

Washington set out to prove that a republic could do more than prevail in war—that it could *endure*. How did he manage it? How did he carry off this bold experiment as if it were a formal ritual? The clearest and most eloquent explanation may lie, not in scholarly analyses, or in Washington's own weighty prose, but in the music of his time. Listen to Haydn and hear the contest between theme and counter-theme, the folk melodies that are given free play but not enough to overpower the final triumph of decorum. Listen to Mozart and hear the stately minuet transformed into a lively rondo, then brought back again to balance and moderation. So with Washington's leadership.

George Washington would lead a revolution and put down a mutiny. He would prosecute a war for independence, and later declare neutrality for the same purpose. He would preside over the creation of a new, complex constitutional scheme full of verbal artifice—without saying a word. As president he would listen to equal but opposite counsel, make his decision, then implore the adviser whose counsel he regularly rejected (Mr. Jefferson) to remain in his cabinet. He would put down a full-scale rebellion without making a single conciliatory gesture, then hand out pardons all around.

Washington's now distant music is really a familiar eighteenth-century medley. Themes and counter-themes. Folk tunes and acquired formalities. Then the final triumph of balance and stability. Washington's policies changed, but never his grand and civil vision of what could be.

If this is a young country, it is an old, old republic as the species goes. Its very first words rang with dignity, permanence, age. The French are now on their fifth republic, and the Soviet Union and Eastern Europe totter into freedom again, while the first and only American republic marches along toward its tricentennial.

What is the key to the remarkable longevity of the American experiment? Those seeking an explanation would do well to study Washington. They might also listen to Haydn's Symphony No. 88 or Mozart's Violin Concerto No. 5, each of which could be dedicated to George Washington.

The well-calculated spirit of Washington is the spirit of republican government. His is still a standard to which, in his phrase, the wise and honest may repair. In this mass democracy that the republic has become, dignity and decorum still have a certain sentimental appeal, but they are scarcely recognized as what they are: guarantees of freedom's permanence.

In a perceptive essay, the historian Edmund S. Morgan pointed out two guiding themes in Washington's politics: interest and honor. The old general understood that republics must appeal to both if they are to endure. It is clear enough that politicians know how to appeal to our interests; American politics today consists of little else. Even when they say "No," contemporary leaders have learned to make it sound like "Yes." But what, we might ask on this Washington's Birthday, has happened to the appeal to honor?

February 19, 1990

49 Rebecca West

A Different Order of Clarity

The first thing the obituaries seemed to mention about Rebecca West was that she was a feminist. ("Famed Writer, Feminist, 90, Dies in London.") It's something one may know, dimly, but it's not the first thing that would occur to those who have read her through the years and decades with delight and gain. Perhaps that is testimony to how effective a feminist she was: her writing had no gender.

The incidental intelligence in her obituary, like that in her prose, is striking—how she was born in Ireland on Christmas Day, 1892, the third daughter of a ne'er-do-well army officer and war correspondent; her days as an aspiring actress and how she took the name Rebecca West from the strong-willed heroine of Ibsen's *Rosmersholm*; her becoming drama critic of the *Evening Standard* at 17, and continuing to write her regular review for the *Telegraph* at 90; how she edited *Freewoman*, a feminist journal her mother wouldn't allow in the house; her affair at 20 with the much older H. G. Wells and its result, Anthony West, novelist and critic . . .

But all that seems secondary, tertiary, of no importance compared to how she wrote, which was like a dream. That is, she wrote with fluid ease and power, and with a wholly different order of clarity that instructed as it fascinated. Under her sway, written words became like the biblical perception of a dream—fraught with meaning and prophecy, judging past and future, full of telling detail.

She could have been a novelist and, for a brief and less important period, was one. Her novels are fine. But they are not why the world values Rebecca West so highly. As a novelist, she had mastered a well-modulated loquacity, like an English gentlewoman speaking endlessly and interestingly in a country garden at twilight without ever raising her voice. As a novelist, she still had something of Cicely Isabel Fairfield—the name she was given at birth, so redolent of all Rebecca West wasn't. She was no more Cicely Fairfield than George Orwell was Eric Blair.

Like George Orwell, Rebecca West set out to explain the world, or all she explored of it, to herself, and in the process to anyone who read her. That is why her reportage was her best work, and why her masterpiece *Black Lamb and Grey Falcon*—a travel book—turned out to be the most prescient, the most historical, and the most clarifying political work of the thirties.

Rebecca West saw the role of the artist as rendering experience anew, clarifying and focusing it. She personified the artist as teacher. In that role, like Orwell, she was able to articulate things that every decent person might know or sense about the world, but that had not been said before. Orwell had the same quality. If decency was Orwell's highest value, Rebecca West's was life. Informed by a religious sensibility, she was constantly choosing life. She was a celebrant of D. H. Lawrence and the author of perhaps the most damning yet admiring study of Saint Augustine in Western letters. ("Every phrase I read of his sounds in my ears like the sentence of my doom and the doom of my age.")

Like Orwell, Rebecca West was a fancier of the English murder. Orwell mourned its decline. No reader of Rebecca West would have, because she could write a murder story like no one else, making it a piece of political and social commentary as well. Her best, "Mr. Setty and Mr. Hume," should be required reading in journalism courses, right from the first, capturing sentence: "The murder of Mr. Setty was important, because he was so unlike the man who found his headless and legless body . . ."

She would go on to examine *The Meaning of Treason* at a time, 1949, when Joe McCarthy was just beginning to smudge the American scene. Her conclusions could have been penned by Learned Hand. Among them:

The traitor can change the community into a desert haunted by fear, and it is our business to realize what force is at work and change it back again. Loyalty has always had its undramatic but effective answer to treason, insisting on its preference for truth instead of deceit, and good faith instead of bad. But on occasion the answer has to be framed more cleverly than at other times, and ours is a period when it becomes no answer at all, but a pact with treachery, if it be not dictated by caution and fastidiousness. We must reject evil and dispel suspicion without falling into the error of confusing unpopular forms of virtue with evil.

And also:

Since the traitor's offence is that he conspires against the liberty of his fellow countrymen to choose their way of life, we ally ourselves with him if we try to circumvent him by imposing restrictions on the liberty of the individual which interfere with the legitimate business of his soul.

Rebecca West also wrote the best modern treatise (except for Orwell's) on the emptiness and tedium of revenge—her commentary on the Nuremberg trials, which begins:

There rushes up towards the plane the astonishing face of the world's enemy: pine woods on little hills, grey-green glossy lakes, too small ever to be anything but smooth, gardens tall with red-tongued beans, fields striped with copper wheat, russet-roofed villages with headlong gables and pumpkin-steeple churches that no architect over seven could have designed.

If Benjamin Cardozo had had a better prose style, and his was not bad, his critique of Nuremberg might have resembled Rebecca West's conclusion:

The ten men slowly choked to death. Ribbentrop struggled in the air for twenty minutes. Yet it would be treachery against truth not to concede that justice was done. Each of these men who had been hanged had committed crimes for which he would have had to give his life under German law; and it would have then been an axe that killed him. But there are stenches which not the name of justice or reason or the public good, or any other fair word, can turn to sweetness.

Like Cardozo, one can respect or even love the law, yet know that it does not contain ultimate or sometimes even seemly answers. Her admirers say Rebecca West raised journalism to an art; what she did was raise it to journalism.

Rebecca West had no sure answers to offer; she saw herself as another tightrope walker—like man in history, bending this way and that, sometimes confidently, never certainly, but elevated and stirring in his curious passage, in his search for balance and for something more, high above the abyss.

March 23, 1983

50 C. Vann Woodward

The Quiet Southerner

The Pulitzer Prize committee honored itself by awarding the 1982 Pulitzer in history to Comer Vann Woodward—Arkansas boy, American scholar, and the quintessential quiet Southerner. If Southern historians could be divided into two broad classes—and they can't be, any more than Southerners themselves can—C. Vann Woodward would epitomize one of two schools.

The other school stretches back to Jefferson Davis and includes those unreconstructed thinkers of the twenties called the Fugitives. Its shibboleth, whether expressed concisely on license plates or bound at length in leather, is some form of: Forget, Hell! This is the school that is always peering over its shoulder at an ever receding past, sporadically vowing to restore it, rumbling like a volcano that erupts at ever less frequent intervals. Its style is by turns scholarly and unlettered, slovenly and eloquent, decadent and noble, but always distinctive. Call it High Southern. It springs from the South of the broadsword virtues. Regardless of its dress or manners or language, its ethos is aristocratic—with the aristocrat's fine disdain for what passes these days for reality. And it has never had any difficulty outshouting the Vann Woodwards.

One need never have met, or even read, Vann Woodward to know him and his school; it is necessary only to have grown up in the South. Dr. Woodward is the quiet man in the barber shop who only listens while others are arguing loudly, or more often agreeing loudly about the latest perfidy of the Yankees and Liberals, those interchangeable categories. The quiet Southerner waits his turn,

176

listening, absorbing, judging without a word or sign of judgment, growing old judging until he can tell what all the participants in the roaring discussion will say, and why they will say it, and for how long they will say it, and why it may not matter.

If Ecclesiastes had been a Southerner and (if Gentle Reader will forgive the impertinence) a shade less free with his opinions and advice, then that writer might have been very much like C. Vann Woodward. Such seers hold things together without forcing them together; they do not command, but they lead others to their own conclusions; they do not prophesy, but they do see right through a lot of things, and without making any celebratory noises about it.

C. Vann Woodward has seen, and told, much. In *Tom Watson: Agrarian Rebel*, he wrote the classic case study of the Populist progression, or regression, in the American South. He traced the politics of Georgia's Tom Watson from idealistic reformer to hate-filled demagogue without ever preaching.

Vann Woodward's beautifully concise *The Burden of Southern History* remains the most eloquent monument to his understanding of the sorrowful but redemptive qualities of Southern history. There is a marvelous dispassion to this book—this tract, really—and it speaks more knowingly and movingly to the reader than all the bunting-wrapped prose of professional Southerners. After all these works and discoveries, what advice, someone asked him, did he have for young people? Dr. Woodward politely declined to mount the pedestal. His response was in the spirit of the quiet observer waiting his turn in the barber shop: "After forty years of teaching, I made it a rule to never offer in general any moral counsel, particularly to young people. Early on, I decided to let them go to Hell in their own way." Which is as much as any wise man can do. Ecclesiates might nod in agreement.

It was The War, that rock from which we are hewn, that left Southern civilization or its residue divided into those two parties—the shouters and the thinkers. And it is assuring to realize that C. Vann Woodward, no common man, is not an uncommon phenomenon in these latitudes. There have always been those who could ride out history, and those forever fixed in its tumultuous wave.

Reese Cleghorn, newspaperman and Georgia boy, wrote a marvelous remembrance entitled "My Grandfather and the Cyclone."

The Cyclone was The War, or maybe all the wild changes that came after it over the course of a century. The story begins, "My Grandfather Reese would have been a hundred years old. He died, still ruddy-faced and pridefully careful about his splash of white Edwardian mustache, less than four months short of the mark. Some of us thought he did not really want to make it; if he did, there would have been a commotion."

And it is commotion that the Vann Woodwards have been patiently, arduously engaged in understanding and impounding for the rest of us, erecting a quiet bulwark of reason and imagination against the malice of time. They love the South no less for their restraint; they simply look at her differently—as a lady who would be offended by loud voices. Flamboyance is not their way. They are neither for nor against it; they just don't see its point. They know, with Shakespeare, that they love least who let men know their love. And yet they reveal that love in every word, and in every silence. That, too, is an inescapable part of the burden of Southern history, and of its redemption.

When Walker Percy won his National Book Award years back, he was asked why the best writers now seemed to come from the South, and he replied: "Because we lost The War." Flannery O'Connor, one of those Southern writers, elaborated on Percy's thesis: "He didn't mean by that simply that a lost war makes good subject matter. What he was saying was that we have had our Fall. We have gone into the modern world with an inburnt knowledge of human limitations and with a sense of mystery which could not have developed in our first state of innocence—as it has not sufficiently developed in the rest of our country." C. Vann Woodward put that same theme into historical terms in his *The Burden of Southern History*.

In a beautiful and austere phrase, Saint Augustine once defined art as "reason in the making." C. Vann Woodward's work and love demonstrate how Southern history can be grace in the making.

April 25, 1982

Index of Names

179